PENGUIN BOOKS

LOOK UP FOR *YES*

Julia Tavalaro was born in 1935. She lived in a New York City public hospital for thirty years before moving to the nursing home where she now lives in Woodmere, New York, on Long Island. She continues to write poetry and has published her work in *The New York Times* and the *Los Angeles Times Magazine*.

Richard Tayson was born in California in 1962 and was educated at Colorado State University and New York University. His poems have appeared in many national magazines, including *The Paris Review*, *The Kenyon Review*, and *Crazyhorse*. Tayson has received *Prairie Schooner*'s Bernice Slote Award and a Pushcart Prize. His first book of poetry, *The Apprentice of Fever*, was chosen by Marilyn Hacker to receive the Stan and Tom Wick Poetry Prize. Richard Tayson lives in New York City and teaches at the New School for Social Research.

JULIA TAVALARO
and RICHARD TAYSON

LOOK UP FOR *YES*

PENGUIN BOOKS

PENGUIN BOOKS
Published by the Penguin Group
Penguin Putnam Inc., 375 Hudson Street,
New York, New York 10014, U.S.A.
Penguin Books Ltd, 27 Wrights Lane,
London W8 5TZ, England
Penguin Books Australia Ltd, Ringwood,
Victoria, Australia
Penguin Books Canada Ltd, 10 Alcorn Avenue,
Toronto, Ontario, Canada M4V 3B2
Penguin Books (N.Z.) Ltd, 182–190 Wairau Road,
Auckland 10, New Zealand

Penguin Books Ltd, Registered Offices:
Harmondsworth, Middlesex, England

First published in the United States of America by Kodansha America, Inc. 1997
Reprinted by arrangement with Kodansha America, Inc.
Published in Penguin Books 1998

1 3 5 7 9 10 8 6 4 2

"Anger" first appeared in *Breakthough*. "Hayfield in the Ocean,"
"A Modern Concentration Camp," and "Out There" were published
in the *Los Angeles Times Magazine*. "Death," "Indifference," "Sex," and
"Silent Prayer" first appeared in *The New York Times*.

THE LIBRARY OF CONGRESS HAS CATALOGUED THE HARDCOVER AS FOLLOWS:
Tavalaro, Julia, 1935–
Look up for yes / Julia Tavalaro and Richard Tayson.
p. cm.
ISBN 1-56836-171-8 (hc.)
ISBN 0 14 02.7282 8 (pbk.)
I. Tavalaro, Julia, 1935– —Health. 2. Quadriplegics—New York (State)—
New York—Biography. I. Tayson, Richard, 1962– II. Title.
RC406.Q33T38 1997
362.4'3'092—dc21   96–48597

Printed in the United States of America
Set in Centaur
Designed by Laura Hough

DEDICATED TO OUR PARENTS

Mary Augustine
Kathryn Beresford
Joseph Horwat
Virgil Dean Tayson

and

to Rick Meyer, who was there all along.

Welcome to my voice of silence.

Life is a precious shell.

Hold it for as long as you can.

Remember, it is only a shell

Which contains the powerful mind.

It says you can do anything,

Be anything.

So say what you will say.

Contents

Foreword xi

Prologue 3

Chapter One   A MODERN CONCENTRATION CAMP   7

Chapter Two   OUT THERE   24

Chapter Three   HALLELUJAH MARRIAGE   43

Chapter Four   BREATHING   66

Chapter Five   DEATH I   77

Chapter Six   SILENT PRAYER   85

Chapter Seven   SUCK IT IN AND SPIT IT OUT   96

Chapter Eight   DREAMING YOU   113

Chapter Nine   WISH   125

Chapter Ten   FACE IN THE MIRROR   136

Chapter Eleven   POEM IN MIND   155

Chapter Twelve   HAYFIELD IN THE OCEAN   187

Epilogue   213

Foreword

In October 1991, when I was hired to teach a writing workshop at Goldwater Memorial Hospital, I met Julia Tavalaro. The first day I saw her, she was confined to a wheelchair, her body upright and her thin legs stretched out before her. A wooden sign dangled on a screw above her head: "My name is Julia. I am nonspeaking. I look up for yes. Ask me ward/floor." She was upset, in pain, and screaming in great gulps of air. Though the degree of her disability filled me with many feelings—fear, sorrow, pity, thankfulness at being able to walk and speak—I could somehow see past the surface level of her disability.

Though Julia was my "student," during that semester I often felt that our roles were reversed. I found her to be fascinating, articulate, able-minded, and, when she wasn't in pain, brimming with every possible emotion, including joy. Though it had been recommended that we designate one hour per week for working together outside of class, that amount soon increased dramatically. During our transcription sessions, we became shy acquaintances, then friends.

We'd discuss subjects as various as poetry, food, suicide, love, sex, music, and family. I marveled that Julia felt things so deeply and that she seemed afraid of nothing. Though we were separated in age by more than twenty-five years, we discovered that we had important things in common.

To write this book, letter by letter, seemed a near impossibility when we began. It sometimes took us an entire day to unravel one of Julia's memories. With great patience, she would spell out events that had happened forty and fifty years before. I was stunned at the degree of precision she brought to the task. She could remember things from so long ago! And when she didn't have an answer to my seemingly endless questions, she would reply with a simple, I D-O-N-T K-N-O-W. I loved her honesty and her humor, her ability with language and her tenacity.

For over a year, Julia wrote prose about her life on her augmentative device, printing out long, narrow rolls of text. When I would walk into her room and pick up her alphabet card, she would simply spell, T-H-E B-O-O-K. I would transcribe this work onto a computer, then return to read aloud what she had written. From her writings, we culled the basic elements of her life story. She'd give me the necessary factual information, and I'd work at home, honing in on the lyrical sensibility I found in her poems. I used the basic structure of her prose, recurring words of her vocabulary, and colloquial phrases that she had grown up with.

I wrote draft after draft, and Julia corrected them all. If anything was inaccurate, she would let me know in no uncertain terms. She accomplished this task under conditions that most writers would find deplorable. She was often in pain or ill or angry. But nearly every time I went to see her, she'd have new writing to give me.

As much as I aided Julia in writing her story, she helped me understand what it's like to live with major disabilities and to struggle steadfastly to make your dreams come true. I am in awe of the will that has kept this woman alive. I have deep respect for her moral and personal integrity, her ability to create, and her never-give-up spirit. Julia Tavalaro has given me an image of persistence that I will never forget. I am grateful.

RICHARD TAYSON
Brooklyn, New York, 1996

Special Thanks To:

The NYU/Goldwater Hospital writing workshops, Minato Asakawa, Arlene Kraat, Deborah Baker, Joyce Sabari, Joan Bennettson, John Urda, Robert Uruma, Linda Tropiano, Peter Meiland, Alexandra Babanskyj, Sharon Sharp, Nancy Levitin, and Deloris Cook.

LOOK UP FOR *YES*

Prologue

For most of my life I have awakened early—sometimes before dawn—to be the first in the house to see sunlight stream through the window near my bed. As a child, I'd turn onto my side and the first thing I'd see was the shack in our backyard that housed my father's automobile repair shop. Beyond that, a huge oak tree stood in the Skpansky's yard. To a seven-year-old girl, that tree appeared awesome, lording over not only the Skpansky's house behind ours but the Anderson's place next door on John Street in Inwood, Long Island.

From my second-story window, I would see the first light appear, seemingly out of nowhere, as if that tree itself had the power to dispel darkness and bring in the new day. Slowly, the sun's rays would gather a ring of gray mist in the oak's branches, pooling light around the tree, creating a spectacle in greens and whites and soft yellows. I would lie in bed, hearing the regular rhythms of my sister Joan breathing beside me, feeling the sheet against my skin and the warm comfort of the blankets. I would imagine, in a childish way, that tree sending its green foliage into my bed—up from my small feet, through my knees and legs, up to my tummy and arms, neck, lips, eyes, sprouting generous leafage like hair over my head.

Even at age seven, I wanted to be better than everyone else, more beautiful than my sisters and the other girls in Public School no. 2, stronger than the boys, a better rifle shot than even my father. From as early as I can remember, I wanted to be the best.

When the best eluded me, I'd use my imagination. If Grandma Horwat forbade me to climb the heights of the Skpansky's oak tree and gave me a doll's carriage instead, I'd lie in bed and close my eyes and pretend to drive that carriage to the oak, where I'd manage the construction of an imaginary tree house, which became famous throughout Nassau County for its special rooms: a makeup room full of mirrors and luxurious dresses, a room with a golden telephone set on a glass table where I'd spend the days conversing with Gene Autrey and Zsa-Zsa Gabor, a trophy room where Father's prize deer heads crowded the walls. Last of all was my favorite: the comic-book room, where I entertained guests with *Superman* and *Tarzan*.

By this time in my reverie, Joan would be waking up beside me, and Midge, my youngest sister, would stir on her couch-bed beside the window. We'd creep out of our room, careful not to wake my father, and tiptoe downstairs to make breakfast. If it was summer, we'd spend the day climbing onto each others' backs and into the oak's branches, swinging down as if we were circus performers. We'd imagine ourselves leaping from high wires onto elephants' backs, twisting in the air, spinning pirouettes and landing on the ground, sometimes with a thud strong enough to knock the wind out of us.

One day Joan climbed so high into the oak tree that I stared in envy at her skill. She stopped and sat on a branch, her legs dangling into the air. "Hey, Julie, watch how far I can fly," she yelled.

I looked up in time to see her drop like a stone, landing on her back with a sound of bone hitting wood. She didn't get up but lay slumped against the bottom of the tree. Midge ran to the house, and by the time Mom came out, Joan was screaming. I yelled, "Joanie's been crucified!" and Mom swore in Polish. "Jezus Chrystus. O moj boze [Oh my god]," she said, reaching down to pull Joan from a nail that had gouged into her back. Joan's screams rang in the air, and as Mom turned her around, I saw a deep gash running from her neck halfway down her spine. Blood stained the tree and made a trail of quarter-sized dark spots all the way to the house. Though she may have needed stitches, Mom soaked her in the tub and swabbed the wound with iodine, saying she didn't have money to pay a doctor. Each time Joanie screamed, I winced and felt the pain as if it were my own.

The next day my father and Mr. Skpansky cut the lower branches off that tree. While the chain saw droned, I mourned the loss of those branches and felt as though my own arms and legs were being amputated, leaving stumps and the smell of wood shavings, dust in the air, my sister's blood.

Now, with sixty years of living under my belt—thirty of them without the use of my arms, legs, or voice—I still wake up early each day. But instead of turning on my side to see out the window, I lie on my back. To combat the pain, I move the only parts of my body I can, my neck and eyes, and look out my hospital-room window. As I watch the first light bring a view of tomato plants heavy with fruit, then concrete slabs and a cinder-block fence, I think of the poems I've written since I've been paralyzed and the ones I'll write today.

Beyond the fence, I can make out the faint blue of water. What I can't see—but know is there, because of jaunts in my motorized wheelchair—are the plumeria's tongue-shaped leaves, the dual flare of the African desert rose and the flowering maple, the lemon tree's ripe burden, and the summer squash running rampant along the ground. A long time ago, the questions of how I got here and when I got here were a horrible mystery to me. I know more now—the details of a hot summer evening in August 1966 came back gradually—but they don't matter as much as I imagined they would. The answers, I've found, don't begin to scale the larger and more dangerous question of my thirty years' existence in this asylum.

Chapter One

A MODERN CONCENTRATION CAMP

Yes, this is it.
When the name is mentioned we throw a fit.
In this hospital——ugh, no——
Please do not let me be
Tortured in another way;
Only the way to Heaven's a good pay.

Here I lie in my bed
Just as if I were dead,
Hoping wishing Hallelujah praying
That my last breath will be my next.

When I awoke
I was still in the same old hoax.
My body was the same:
Wanting to move.
I had no voice, only a hole for breathing.

Tubes in all parts of me
Told me
This was
The beginning
Of The End.

Slowly, the air lightens. All around is mist and a blue-gray fog. I am awake and not awake. I don't think I have eyes, but I can see myself on a mountain covered with zigzag lines. I try to follow the pattern and climb up. With each step I slide down, farther from the mountain's peak. The air melts into deep purple, then orange, then tan. A multitude of voices swarms around me, and I can't decide if I want to go up into the sun or down into darkness below the stones.

The light changes to a blanket of silver mist. The mountain's hugeness scares me. I'm afraid no one will find me. I lie down in the dirt and cry because I'm exhausted, going nowhere.

Everything is still. Then I hear voices buzzing around me, one more shrill than the rest. A woman's voice. Loud. Close to me. Near where my head used to be.

"Fuck! Goddamn," she says.

The mist evaporates. I can feel only a tightness in my body, a stricture. Something is very wrong.

My mind surfaces, slowly. A deep fear grips me. I do not open my eyes. I feel a sadness well up in the empty nothingness of my body. I start to cry, but no sound comes, no tears flow. My mind tries to put things together, but it feels like the connectives are missing.

I panic. In desperation, my mind starts to work faster. I try to scream. Again, I can't make a sound. Where are my screams? If I can hear the woman's angry words, why can't I hear my own voice? Then, like a revelation in a nightmare, it dawns on me: I am dead.

I try to lift my right hand, but it's rigid, inflexible, strapped to my chest like a dead person's. I attempt to unclench my left fist, but it's as hard and unbending as stone. I struggle to move my feet—and can't. Once more, I try to scream to convince myself that I'm alive. No sound comes forth, and I hear only the gnashing of teeth in my head.

This is what death must feel like: You cry silently and no one notices. You try to lift an arm, only to find you've turned to stone. You howl inaudibly into the silence. No one comes. You do this for eternity.

Suddenly, I remember Judy, my lovely fourteen-month-old daughter. Where is she? Why do I imagine her crying? I remember she'd been giggling and playing in her high chair after dinner while I stacked the dishes in the washer. I'd had one of my headaches, a bad one, and as I stood in front of the dishwasher, I felt another coming on. I wanted to get Judy to bed right away so I could lie down. I carried her upstairs and gave her a bath. But she wasn't crying then, so why do I remember that now?

I think back, piecing memories together. I remember

drying her off, then sprinkling her with baby powder and watching the dust rise in the air. It reminded me of fog, the kind you can't see through. My headache kept getting worse—it felt like someone was slicing off the crown of my head with a sheet of glass. I lifted Judy off the dressing table and put her yellow pajamas on her. I laid her in her crib and gave her a pacifier.

I have a hard time remembering what happened next. I replay the events in my mind. After leaving her room, I turned to go downstairs—yes, I remember the gold carpet beneath my feet—and as I made the first step, Judy started to cry. It was unusual for her to fuss like this. I thought milk would help settle her, so I started to go downstairs to heat some. I remember my hand on the banister, my husband, George, downstairs watching television, Judy's high-pitched wails—but everything is hazy after that. Once again, with an escalating sense of dread, I try to remember.

I am in the kitchen, standing in front of the stove, an empty bottle on the counter. As the milk heated, I heard Judy's cries. The walk back to her was difficult. Each step up required effort. Even before I reached the landing, I was out of breath. My headache got worse with each cry. At the top of the stairs I turned right to go to Judy's crib.

As soon as I gave her the bottle, she stopped crying. My head felt like it was going to explode, but all I could think of was how I wanted to finish the dishes so I could rest. Satisfied that Judy was no longer crying, I returned to the top of the stairs.

. . .

The woman cussing turns on what sounds like my father's chain saw adjusted to its lowest setting. This sound next to my ear scares me even more. The woman stands by my bed, and though I'm still afraid to open my eyes, I can tell she's fumbling with something.

Then I open my eyes. The first thing I see is a woman in a white uniform and a white cap. Though my neck feels stiff, I can turn slightly to see a sleeve against dark skin. The sleeve looks starched, too white. Its brightness hurts my eyes, as does the light above the woman's head. I realize this is a nurse. I know I'm not dead.

I can move my neck forward about an inch, just enough to see a sheet pulled up to my abdomen. If I slant my eyes down, I can see that my arms, bent at the elbows, lie pinned to my chest. Each hand is balled up in a tight, relentless fist. Each of my thumbs lies curled beneath my fingers. I have a sensation of pain in my lower extremities, as if vermin keep gnawing my left leg. It feels as though someone has hammered my left knee down to where my shin used to be, then twisted it forty-five degrees to the left. There is a sensation of hot, then ice cold, from the left side of my hip down to my twisted toes.

On the wall across from my bed, the sky is darkening. I look toward the thickening night and call for my daughter, my husband, my parents. No sound comes. Though their names are clear in my mind, I can't induce my lips, tongue, and breath to voice them. Each name comes out the same: a protracted howl that only I can hear.

The nurse drops the silver can. "Fuck! Goddamn," she

says, retrieving the can from the floor, then finally opening it. She holds it in her hand and walks toward me. The nurse doesn't seem to see me looking at her, trying to get her attention by moving my head from side to side and rotating my eyes.

She turns a dial on the machine beside me and pours the contents of the can into a container hanging from a metal pole. That's when I feel two tubes, one in my nose, the other in my throat. I see the liquid go into the machine that pumps it out a tube that runs across my sheets and snakes up into my nose. As the liquid goes into my nostril, I look at the nurse concentrating on the machine. I feel like killing her.

I notice three other beds in the room, all of which are occupied. Someone in the bed across from mine is babbling so loudly I can hear her over the sound of the feeding machine. The whites of her eyes pointing toward the ceiling, she sits up in her bed and mumbles in a gibberish like the pig Latin Joanie and I used to sing to get our mother's goat. "Foo seee like lee. Foo seee like lee. And who knows the way back home." Another nurse leans over the woman and tells her to eat her dinner. But the babbling continues, and in the middle of that nonsense sound, a man wearing a white duster walks into the room.

Right away, I figure he's a doctor and I must be under his care. He speaks in a language as foreign as the woman's babbling. Though I can tell it's English, I don't recognize most of the words. As soon as he looks at me, I think, he'll know I'm awake and arrange to get me out of here. But he only says a few words to the nurse feeding me, then leaves as quickly as he came.

I watch the tube fill up, propelling the liquid toward me. I'd like to get out of bed and go home. I try to slide onto my elbow and hoist my body up so the nurse will know I'm awake. I want to walk away with the people I hear moving in what sounds to be a corridor outside the room, but my left leg doesn't feel like it's there. I see my right leg in front of me, just beneath the sheet, but when I think *move*, it does nothing. Something drips down my throat, and I wonder what month it is.

Now I'm horrified. I want to reach for my voice in my throat, but my arms won't move. I know I have a throat and should be able to scream for someone to come take me away. I realize there is no power in my legs, arms, hands, voice, body. I realize that I am paralyzed.

The woman with starched clothes bends over me to wipe away some liquid she spilled on my chin. She presses down hard, the way a maid scrubs a stain from a carpet. In reaction to her harsh touch, I make a deep whining sound, like a dog's warning growl. The nurse stops and holds the cloth in the air in front of her. As she looks at me, her face registers a perplexed expression, and she tilts her head, contemplating the sound I've just made. Then she balls up the cloth and barks, "Shut up, you crybaby!" She goes to the sink, wrings out the cloth, looks at herself in the mirror, turns away, and without looking back at me, leaves the room.

My mind floats up toward the light. I can see myself

stretched out rigid in the hot, humid air, the light shining around me. I see the mountain once again. As the mist thickens around it, the mountain transforms into a series of hills, each one laced with zigzag lines. I dream I'm digging my hands into the wet earth, struggling for something to hold on to. A voice in my mind calls out for my father, and I wake up, terrified, for my first night back on earth.

. . .

My father, Joseph Horwat, was born in Budapest, Hungary, in 1908 and immigrated to Pittsburgh, Pennsylvania, when he was a boy. Though he never talked much about himself, I know from hearsay that he was a dashing young man who kept his thick brown hair slicked back in the style of the thirties and who had dark blue eyes, full lips, and a muscular build. He liked to joke and dance and race stock cars, never caring one jot for what other people thought. He had a scathing sense of humor and would sometimes become violent, his temper turning on a dime as he took off his black belt and gave one of his four children a strapping while the others hid in the backyard, behind the woodpile.

As family legend has it, my father was one of fourteen children, all of whom were born in a Gypsy caravan. He attended school until the sixth grade, when he went to work with his father in the coal mines of Pittsburgh. After a foreman discovered his knack for fixing machines, my father was promoted to car repairman. He met and married my mother in 1933 and drove her on his motorcycle from Pittsburgh to Inwood, Long Island, one of the five larger towns in Nassau County.

He rented a house on Wheelock Street, where the basements were built high enough to avoid flooding from the salt marshlands. Since Inwood was an undesirable place to live back then, only a few other houses, most of them rented by immigrants, dotted the street. The view from our front window was of the brickyard across the street and the wide expanse of marshlands. This was the house where I was born on January 31, 1935.

In 1939 my father bought a house a few miles away at Eighty-four John Street, another immigrant enclave. The people who lived nearby, along Mott Avenue, Wahl Avenue, and Roosevelt Street, were mostly Italians. My parents found themselves outcasts. They were lucky in one respect: two other non-Italian families shared the corner of our block. The Skpanskys, a Polish family whose girls befriended my sisters and me, lived directly behind us. The Andersons, a black family who had preceded the Italians, lived next door.

As soon as we'd moved to John Street, my father converted our garage into his mechanic's shop and our backyard into a junkyard. Even with the most sinister of hangovers, he was up before dawn, coffee cup in one hand, wrench in the other, heading out the back door and across the gravel drive to his shop.

Sometimes, he would let me into his smudged and tarnished world of deflated tires, crusted chassis, distributor caps, brake shoes, and cracked radiators. It was here, in his paradise of the imperfect, in the whiskey smell of him and the bloody-knuckle feel of him, that I learned not only to love but to identify with his competitive spirit. Something in the glow of his eyes as he polished a car with wide swaths of the chamois cloth transfixed me during those long afternoons in his shop with the radio on and Maurice Chevalier singing in the hot, electric air.

Most of the time, I'd sit and watch his calm, steady hands strip copper wiring or grip a pair of pliers. I'd see the look of determination on his face as he stood at his greasy workbench, and I'd marvel at his intense concentration on a tiny metal part in the palm of his hand. He'd hum to himself and sometimes make small talk or tell me what he was doing. But most of the time we remained silent. When I did ask a question, he'd complete his task before answering softly, under his breath, his Hungarian accent becoming fainter and fainter through the years.

By the time I was eight, I'd imagined myself driving stock cars like my father. Or I'd be the hunter who came down off the mountain with a stiffened deer tied to my shoulders, the one who strung it from a hook at the top of our garage and gutted it right there, never squirming before the blood. And I'd have his humor. Like the time he hung a gutted deer on a rope over our garage and cut the buck's three-point antler from its head and put it on like a fantastic cap of hide, bone, and blood and laughed until Mom came out of the house to snap a picture. Yes, I wanted my father's spine.

I got it all: his cunning and persistence, his daring and foolhardiness. All those summer days in my father's shop, with his pint of whiskey hidden in the nail drawer and the sounds of music, electric saws, and engines made him mine. The neighbors on John Street used to tell me how much I resembled him—the long, lanky legs; the balanced, narrow face with high cheekbones; the serious intent of my locked jaw; the caustic humor.

In my mind's eye I have a window my father some-times comes to. He usually has a gun in his hand—a pistol or the rifle he used to hunt with—a half-grin on his face, and a racer's beanie on his head. He likes to cross his arms and tuck his fingers into the crook of his elbow. He smells of sweat two days old, has axle grease smeared on his palms, smokes unfiltered Lucky Strike cigarettes, and drinks his whiskey straight. He wears overalls and shirt sleeves and is the one man I'd trust to save my family if the house caught fire.

When I envision him at my window, I see the man who would once in a blue moon hold me affectionately as we listened to Jack Benny on the radio, and tell me I'd grow up and "do him proud." Father never gave me the impres-sion that life would be easy. He made me believe that I could do anything if I worked hard enough and didn't give up at the crucial moment. "No daughter of mine's gonna be a quitter," he'd say.

After the hunter, the motorcycle driver, the skilled mechanic, I see another man—my father in his late fifties, his body fallen at the shoulders, his stomach fattened, his eyes puffed and lined from running his shop in the days and drinking heavily most nights. The skin below his jaw showed as many wrinkles as the coxcomb of a bantam rooster who has had one too many fights, one too many courtship dances. As his body was ravaged by stomach and throat cancer, he refused any doctor's care. Johnny Walker whiskey and mechanic work remained his only medications.

When I look away from the window and close my eyes, I see my father coming home late from John Mayo's bar, arguing loudly with my mother. This is the part of my father I like to recall least, yet it's perhaps more vivid than the rest of him.

I hear him calling her a "Nazi Pollack," yelling that she was thrown out of Kraków because of her bad housekeeping. The slaps begin. I hear the sound of his boots as he goes downstairs, then dishes, whiskey bottles, and chairs being thrown against the walls. I get up, push my sisters Joan and Midge under the beds. But he arrives and drags us out. With bloodshot eyes and a half-sweet, half-putrid smell I'll never forget, he slurs something about me being the oldest and leads me to his gun closet.

At the closet—normally off limits to us—I stand on the threshold of the forbidden. Feeling half excited to be at the edge of my father's sacred world, I am also half afraid that he is expecting something of me, that I'll have to prove my spunk or be cast from his orbit forever. I hear him going through the closet, pulling out his rifles and pistols, cussing and grunting and mumbling under his breath, making the hallway thick with the smell of his drunkenness. I hear Mother crying in her room and Joan and Midge scrambling to get back under the bed.

With face flushed and forehead sweaty, he finally emerges from the closet and proceeds to line up his guns against the wall. Turning to me with a devious expression, he tells me to decide which gun he should use to kill my mother.

I can bear almost all these memories of my father. I can even think with some pleasure of the neighbors calling him "Crazy Joe," the wild Hungarian who could drink anyone under the table, then get up and go to a woman and make such a fool of himself that she'd feel sorry and take him home for the night.

I think I've inherited from him what saved my life—a will strong as the vise at the far end of his worktable, the intrepid Gypsy body, the stubbornness, and the fierce desire to get the job done. But I also fear I've inherited my father's weaknesses—his selfishness, arrogance, and violent temper.

. . .

As I'm waking up the next morning, I see sunlight shining through the window across from my bed. Unlike yesterday,

I am not climbing a mountain to reach the light. I lie un-comfortably still, feeling the sharp ache in my legs, arms, and back. I remember things from yesterday, especially the woman feeding me, and I wonder how long I've been living on liquid food. However long I was asleep before I heard the nurse cussing, I know that I'm alive, and that this is my second day back in the world.

I turn my head an inch to the left, look up at the light, and realize I must have been in a coma. During yesterday's reawakening, it took a long time before I could register the objects in the room, but today I see a blue sky and a half-drawn shade at the window. I know what these things are, just as I recognize the sound of snoring coming from the woman in the bed across from mine. I try to recall what's happened to me. How long was I in a coma, and who put me here? What's happened to make me sleep so deeply?

When I turn my head on my pillow to look toward the snoring woman, the light suddenly changes to mist. My first memory of what had happened comes back sharply.

There was a fog around the staircase the night I gave Judy her bottle and walked back downstairs to finish the dishes. My head was still pounding as I went into the kitchen to load the dishwasher. It felt like someone was hit-ting my skull with a hammer. The dishwasher was still humming, so I walked into the living room. George sat watching television with our new puppy on the couch be-side him.

As my headache got worse, I grew more afraid. My vision began to blur. I went over to the fireplace and put my hands on the mantle to help steady me. I stared at the bricks and the unlit logs. Though it had been over five years since I'd divorced my first husband, Jim, I was still bothered by the fact of our breakup. I wondered if I had caused us to separate. I also worried about the foster kids George and I were adopting. I'd convinced him that we had enough resources to raise the large family I'd always dreamed of. After months of interviews and paperwork, the adoption was nearly finalized. We'd been given permission by the Department of Welfare to adopt two children, a girl and a boy—seven-year-old Joan and four-year-old Frank. They were siblings, and I felt grateful to be able to take them both.

Thinking about these things made my head throb even more. My thoughts turned to Judy's first birthday a few months back, and how next year we'd have the basement room done so Judy, the adopted kids, and George's nieces and nephews could roughhouse all they wanted. I thought of the party favors I'd buy, horns and those noisy New Year's honkers. Then, clear as day, I saw the face of my old flame, whom I'll call André, and heard the voice of my first husband calling me a sex maniac.

I thought I was going crazy, and since my headache was getting worse, I knew I'd better go upstairs for some aspirin. I remember thinking I should have done this earlier, but I had been occupied with Judy. I felt terrified as I walked across the living room and stood at the bottom of the stairs. Unable to move or speak, I seemed frozen. I stood with my hand on the walnut banister and felt the soft carpet under my bare feet.

Everything after that is a blur.

I move my head and see starched dresses, white nylons, a knee, a shaft of light on the floor. Diapers, urine bags, a white gown move across my field of vision. A thermometer is pinched between bony fingers, bed rails appear, and I hear strange cackling noises. A hand moves up to raise the nearby window, and air rushes in for the first time. I want to pull that hand toward me, warm it between my breasts, kiss it in thanks. But I have no sense of possessing lips or breasts or anything but a feeling of pain. I can't ask that hand to help me, to pick up a phone and call my husband to come and take me home. Like last night, no matter how hard I try, my voice won't ask the question.

A white dress comes close to me, lifts me, laughs to another white dress who makes a sucking sound between her teeth and says, "The vegetable needs changing." I realize with sudden terrible knowledge that I am a grown woman about to experience what it's like to be a baby. I imagine I am my father screaming at the nurses. I feel my jaw open, but I can't produce a sound. I feel my hands clench tighter to my chest, every fiber in my body contracts, and I try hard to hit someone. But no part of me moves. When I think I've exhausted all possibilities, my neck pulls up and I groan. I hear myself this time. Though the sound is nasal and muted, the nurses stop chattering.

I can't see the nurse behind me, but the one in front comes into view, and I register, for a second, her face—a kind, brown face with white teeth, pink tongue, red lipstick. She stops pulling the sheets back and stares at me. What a miracle to look into the eyes of another person! What a shock to put cheekbones next to eyes, eyes next to a high forehead that meets black hair. She is human. Her fingers touch my body. I am a human being trying to scream, *"Fuck, goddamn—don't you dare laugh at me."*

The face with red lipstick says, "Ooo, looks like she's feisty today." The voice standing behind this first voice chuckles and says, "I give her six more months—no, three." Then I feel the gown go up my chest, and one of the white, starched sleeves rubs against my face. A hand presses my pelvic bone, and I smell urine. I feel my facial muscles tighten, as if my cheekbones were becoming longer. My eyes sting, and I begin to cry. Neither nurse notices. They pin another sheet diaper on me and lay my body down. Without a word, they leave me alone to stare out my window, my wasteland of sky, my ocean so hard to forget.

Chapter Two

OUT THERE

Where where out there?
I hear a voice
Laughing and giggling
It might be her
Where where out there?
I hear a voice
Moaning crying
It might be her
What's out there?
Sun and tears
Might be rain
Might be the sun
Might be her
What have the dreams meant?
Happiness, I presume.
My ugliness is more like it.

Ah ll morning, I listen to the sound of my breath passing
in and out of the tube in my throat. I lie thinking
about that tube, wondering who put it there. I remember
the gills of the first striped bass I caught the day Father took
me and Joan fishing at the Far Rockaway shore. I was the
first to catch one, and even now I can still feel the heavy line
as I reeled it in and held the rod straight out over the water,
struggling as Father had taught me with my legs firm
against the pull. I landed the fish on the sandy shore and
looped my fingers into its gills and lay the gleaming silver
body on a stone. Joan grimaced as I sank the knife in side-
ways to slit its length open.

Across the room, water drips into a sink. A glass par-
apet separates people walking in the corridor from me, the
lady speaking pig Latin in the bed opposite, and the two
bodies supine in the other beds. At irregular intervals, an
alarm sounds in the hall. It continues screaming until a
hand reaches up on the wall near my door. "Damn patients," a voice says when the alarm shuts off, "wish they'd
stay put. Every time one of them wheels into the main hall,
the friggin' alarm goes off."

I feel a rage so deep it makes my body tremble. I want
to kill anyone who walks near my bed. If no one comes
close, I want to kill myself, to be released from the pain
shooting through my unbending legs. I try to scream, but
only my stifled moan punctuates the seconds ticking heavy
as doom in the room of wasted air.

The babbling voice of the woman across from me gets
louder. "That's *it*, I can't play anymore. Foo seee like lee and

my stomach hurts me." I move my head on the pillow and see her sitting up, her mouth open. Her teeth are missing. I want to punch her hard enough to knock her off her bed. She shakes her head and quietly tears the blue gown off her shoulders. A nurse comes in, sees her doing this, and goes to the doorway. "She's at it again," she shouts at the top of her lungs. "Somebody get in here and help get her back on track!" I must be in a home for mental patients, I think. Am I insane? Why did they put me here?

Hospital? Prison? Asylum? How long have I been asleep, and where is my daughter? I turn and see a nurse pulling the woman's arms over her head, holding her down on the bed, screaming, "Hold still. Just quiet down, will you!" My arms pull tighter against my chest. I realize I don't even know how long I have been here.

I try to recall what I did after I climbed the stairs to get the aspirin. I remember that it was summer, because Judy didn't adjust well to the heat. I worried about her. Maybe that affected my headache, too. Now I remember words slowly, the way someone who has been away from her country remembers the old language upon her return: M-I-L-K, B-O-T-T-L-E, B-A-B-Y, P-A-I-N. I repeat these words as I lie in the light, watching dust rise and settle. Then I hear an anonymous shout, the rustle of starched clothes in the hallway. I don't know what will happen next in this pandemonium, but I feel buried deep in a hole everyone keeps stepping over, not knowing I'm down here, breathing.

Time passes. The woman opposite is now quiet. A

dress with no face comes into the room to feed me. Her head is too high to be in my line of vision. The dress stands by my bed, and a hand appears. It isn't the hand from the night before, but it performs the same task. The hand tears open another silver can. The clear tube fills with beige liquid. The dress doesn't touch me except to turn my head toward the feeding machine droning once again beside me. Hands and parts of people move in and out of sight, but I can't put them together. I keep spelling D-E-A-T-H in my mind, thinking that I don't want to live if I can't move my arms and legs, if I can't speak, if I can't go home.

After the machine rations dinner into the tube connected to my nose, another nurse comes into the room and passes her arm over my face. I see pink roses on her sleeve. As the arm inside the sleeve pulls me forward to hitch up my gown, I smell the pink roses my mother used to grow in our yard back on John Street.

. . .

My mother, Mary Augustine, loved pink roses. She cultivated those flowers as if they were children, her strong hands hollowing out a place in the earth for them to take root. I remember the springtime when, crouched on her knees and stained up to her wrists in wet earth, my mother would empty a bucket of water over the thorny sticks. She worked the dirt with her trowel, staining her housedress, moving from plant to plant, as if nothing mattered so much as making those flowers bloom.

Half Polish and half German, Mom was born in 1901 in Kraków, Poland. Having no formal education, my mother emigrated to Scranton, Pennsylvania, in 1920 and worked as a housemaid until 1933, when she met and married my father. After I was born in 1935, my mother gave birth to my three siblings: Joan in 1937, Midge in 1940, and Joey in 1943. By the time Joey was old enough to walk, our mother wouldn't speak to us about her German ancestry for fear we'd suffer mistreatment at school due to anti-German sentiment. Mother became secretive, more silent than her already reticent nature.

To the people of Inwood, my mother was a beautiful Polish immigrant with dark hair and blue-gray eyes who spoke broken English and could make a five-dollar bill stretch farther than anyone else in the state. She rarely smiled and often appeared uncomfortable in the presence of other people. She'd hold her arms nervously behind her back, glance down at the floor, dip her shoulders and fidget, then turn away to look out a window or brush back a wayward strand of hair. Even at festive times, her face was set, her lips tightly closed, her jaw braced, as if she'd lived through severity of such magnitude that she was determined never to tell of it.

Even though flowers made my mother happy, her face revealed a deep, bitter sadness. Much of her pain had to do with my father's carousing. When he spent his earnings on women and drink, my mother had to use her ingenuity to make ends meet. She could do it, too, because she had a knack for finding great buys at bazaars and rummage sales. She was so skilled that she could outfit the three of us girls for one dollar each, including shoes and stockings and sometimes hats.

We'd bring the clothes home and let Mom show us the proper way to wash the fabrics and press out each wrinkle and arrange the skirt or blouse just so. She'd stand us in front of a mirror, instructing us on how the buttons and zippers had to be in a perfect straight line, and how we could play with colors, mixing and matching purples, reds, and bright mint greens. Joanie and Midge and I would take turns holding dresses in front of us, letting Mom color coordinate an outfit for each day of the week, all the while forgetting that these clothes were secondhand.

Mom also spent a lot of time on our hair. She would curl it herself or teach us how to braid it. She even showed us how to apply lipstick and then pressed a tissue gently to our mouths to blot it. And once when I asked her if I could try some perfume, she said, "No, Julie, that's for *putta* (a word she picked up from the Italians, meaning 'whore'). First thing after perfume is boys get too familiar with their hands."

Before my mother's eyesight became weak because of anemia, she'd go on Friday nights to the Gem Theater, where the owners showed B-grade movies and gave away free dishware. When Mom asked me to stay at home and babysit my sisters, and soon my baby brother, I knew she was going just to get free plates.

We children learned to be ingenious in our own way. Joanie and I were world-class sneaks. And Mother would be in on any conspiracy we could come up with. I remember one time in particular when we had wanted some candy. We waited for Father to fall into one of his drunken slumbers, then drew straws to decide who would crawl on her hands and knees into his room. Joanie lost. While Dad slept, she inched her way to where he'd discarded his pants, knowing exactly which pocket he kept his money in. She snatched the change and gave it to Mom so she could buy bread and milk. For our trouble, Mom gave us three pennies. We skipped down to Coco's, the neighborhood drugstore, for licorice sticks and Mary Janes.

I was not so lucky. Once, after I drew the short straw and had to crawl across the floor, I knocked over a lamp. Dad woke up, saw me holding his pants, and figured us out quickly. He found some of his change missing and gave me such a whipping that I couldn't sit down for two days. From then on, Joan did the pilfering.

My mother's greatest ally in her struggle with my father was Grandma Horwat, whom we called "Nana." Even in her sixties she used to make the trip once or twice a month from Uniontown, Pennsylvania, to our house in Inwood. I was always relieved when she arrived because I knew there would be a respite in my parents' fighting and that Nana would put Dad in his place. There wouldn't be whippings, either. Strange as it seems to me now, that old woman with white hair wound in two long braids piled on her head had the power to rein my father in.

Nana had a stocky body and wore brightly colored housedresses and black shoes that Joanie and I called "Granny shoes." Her hands were wrinkled from doing dishes and laundry and from changing fourteen babies' diapers. What I remember most about Nana are her eyes. They were the most beautiful eyes I'd ever seen—purple, greenish, gray-blue. When she'd hug me and kiss my forehead and try to teach me the Lord's Prayer in my mother's kitchen, I'd stare into those eyes, thinking they'd convey whatever I needed to know.

Even as an eight-year-old I believed in reincarnation. When I'd tell Nana about my belief, she would screw up her face and stare at me with those remarkable eyes and say, "Posh, Julie. Who put those crazy ideas into your head? You must always remember to go to church on Sundays." Never wondering why I believed I'd known Nana before, I would smile and let her hold me.

I recall vividly one time when Dad whipped us and Mom phoned Nana afterward. Nana came down that very day and marched into our house, had a few words with Mom, then went straight out to Dad's shop. I stood at the upstairs window and saw the most amazing scene: a white-haired woman yelling at my brazen father, doubling up her fist and going at him until her braids came undone and fell onto her shoulders. I can still hear her yelling, "If you ever whip those kids again, I'll wrap that belt around your neck and hang you from the rafters!" That did the trick: from then on Dad refrained from whipping us.

After Nana left my parents continued to fight. When

I wanted to escape their arguments, I would go into the front yard, where I could watch the street and smell Mother's roses. They grew in such profusion that they reached up the side of our house and over the roof and made a wave of pink riot along the windows and front trellis.

Once, while I was out in the yard, I heard my father screaming at my mother. I cringed at the anger in his voice. But something in me rebelled against her grimness, too. I had my nose in a flower when Dad flew out of the house in a rage, bounded down the porch steps, and grabbed me by the shoulders. "Come with me, Julie. We're going to show your mother a thing or two." He took me out back, into his junkyard of heaped metal car parts and on into his shop. He reached up to a top shelf, pulled down a box of lye, and told me to take it outside. He followed me out the door with a bucket of kerosene and led me to the front yard. His face flushed with anger, he silently stirred kerosene into the lye and told me to pour it over my mother's roses. I was glad to watch the healthy leaves, the quickening buds, the full flowers absorb that poison. In a few days those beautiful flowers lay heaped, wilted, and dead on the front lawn.

. . .

The nurse with the pink roses on her sleeve sings as she removes my diaper. She lifts me from the front, hitching up the blue gown, and leans me back on the mattress, face up. I keep looking at the faded roses on her sleeve, thinking my mother is down there somewhere. I tilt my eyes up and see part of her face as she takes the diaper from between my legs. She doesn't speak to me or look me in the face to see if I'm alive, and I suddenly realize that I'm not going to get better. I'm just going to get worse. The nurse, singing softly about a daydream believer and a homecoming queen in a voice thick as honey, is waiting for me to die.

She stops singing and calls another nurse into the room. "Now we'll show you the ropes about showers," she says. "Number one: Don't let any of 'em tell you how they want it done. You're boss, and don't you forget it. This one doesn't got a brain. Can't do nothin' but cry, so don't mind her."

The two of them undo my diaper and untie my hospital gown—sky-blue cotton, four sizes too large. I think of how I used to spend hours washing and ironing, stitching and mending, just to look my best for the boys. One pair of hands unbuttoning me has pearl fingernail polish on, and I think of how that color used to be my favorite those evenings before bed when I'd sit on the porch and paint my nails until they shone.

The nurse with the polish leaves the room and returns, wheeling a strange object behind her. It looks like an ocher-yellow door that's been taken off its hinges and laid flat, six or eight inches off the floor. The nurse is sliding it across the linoleum, so it must have wheels underneath. Strangest of all is the metal drainpipe at one end.

As she wheels it over and stops to the right of my bed,

the other nurse rolls a machine that looks like a metallic crane into the room and says, "You know about the Hoyer lift, right?" The nurse with the polish nods.

"Good," the first nurse says, rolling the cranelike object toward me. I see that it has two chrome rods parallel to the floor and a crank near the top for raising and lowering a third rod that's connected to four chains. The nurses attach the chains to a piece of canvas with S-shaped metal hooks. They don't tell me what they're going to do, but I figure they'll lift me out of bed and transfer me onto that strange yellow stretcher. One nurse leans me as far forward in the bed as my inflexible back will bend, while the other drapes the piece of canvas behind my shoulders. It feels as though they will double me over until my back splits open. Then they lean me back, still with the canvas behind me, so I'm lying flat on the bed. Their hands attach those silver hooks in the holes along the fabric's edge. I feel a wave of fear rise up from the ocean depths of my mind. *Whatever they do, they cannot kill me. It will pass. Whatever they do will pass.*

One of the nurses cranks a handle on the side of the stretcher, and the flat surface rises until it's even with my bed. Without explanation or warning, I'm lifted into the air and maneuvered over the stretcher, then laid face up. As they arrange my feet near the drain pipe, their hands pull my legs and twist my arms, causing sharp spasms of pain to shoot up the length of my left leg. I signal with quick movements of my eyes and slow turns of my head how much it hurts when they touch me. They don't seem to notice. I feel a small sound come into my throat and hear a louder groan spill from my mouth.

The nurses stop. I open my mouth to scream, but no sound comes. The one with the roses looks down at me. "The people they put in this place keep gettin' worse and worse," she shrugs. "Can't even tell if they're human or not, now can you?"

The next thing I know, I'm being wheeled out of the room. For the first time I see the corridor. I can't see much, though, because I'm lying flat on the stretcher. Mostly I'm aware of the icy-colored fluorescent lights and the nurses' legs moving in front and to the side of me. A pair of pants walks by, and I want to see the person's face, but he's moving too fast. Besides the doctor who ignored me yesterday, this is the first man I've seen since I awakened from the coma. Maybe I'm in a hospital for women, I think, cringing at the idea.

I listen carefully as the nurses talk, hoping they'll say the name of a hospital, a street, a town, a year. I try to look for a sign, something that will indicate the hospital's name. I know it's likely I'm either in Queens or Manhattan, and I imagine, by the severity of my condition, that it would be one of the best medical facilities in the country. But I know nothing for sure.

At the end of the corridor, the nurses wheel me into a room I've never seen before. Humidity blankets the air, and as a pair of hands slips into rubber gloves, I smell ammonia. A shower turns on. The gloves lift the gown off me, and I'm struck with a wall of water shooting me in the face, the eyes, the nose, the chest. For a second, I can't breathe. I vainly strain to scream.

My neck is struck by a jet of water, some of which spills into the tube in my throat. I feel as though I'm drowning, like the first time Father pushed me into the water at Far Rockaway Beach and I felt sea salt in my throat and nose. I thought the water would fill my lungs and I'd sink. Then I found that I could move my arms and legs and drift up to my father, who was looking down at me, reaching out his hand to save me.

But in the shower, I can neither move nor speak. I hear the nurses' voices rise over the sound of the water striking the plastic gurney, my skin, and the sea-green tiles around me. The nurse who had been singing yells as she holds up a washcloth.

"I forgot to tell you one thing. Always remember to cover the trach tube with a folded cloth. Don't want her to drown, God forbid!"

She places the cloth over the tube, and I can feel how I have to breathe just from my mouth and nose.

"Now, let's turn her on her side and give that ugly butt of hers a quick squirt."

I feel my body rolled like a piece of dough. One nurse holds my feet while the other pushes my back. They raise me halfway into a sitting position, and just as they're about to turn me over, I see my left hand through the corner of my eyes. I notice my fingers. At first I'm only able to concentrate on how thin each finger is and how tightly they're curled into the flesh of my hand. Then I realize that something is missing: my wedding band. No ring of gold, just marble-colored skin pulled taut around the bones.

I am confused and enraged at the absence of my wedding ring. My first thought is that George had come to the hospital while I was still in a coma and, finding me knotted and twisted and undesirable, had simply slipped the ring off and taken it with him. Then I think it's possible that one of the doctors had removed it in a routine procedure before my hand became bound in its tight fist. However it disappeared, the loss of my ring is symbolic of my husband's absence.

The women roll me over at the shoulder until I feel I will drown and no one will lift a finger to save me. That's when I find a silent place in the back of my mind, where my thoughts can sink and I can find solace in seeing colors pass before me. I drift in that warm place now, swim past a weed here, a shaft of light there, toward a darting red fish and a green haze filtering the blue, the shaft of penetrating light. Color flashes like a strand of jewels across my mother's wrist, and I watch the jewels sink—emerald, ruby, amethyst—each a thought free of pain, a window in a submarine at the bottom of the ocean. Protected, I float and look at my ruby, my diamond, my sapphire, my tunnel of light up, until the nurse cranks the water off and silence prevails.

My breathing resumes. The nurses dry me off with a towel that feels as abrasive as sandpaper. The gown is draped back over me. I feel pain wherever their hands touch me. I suddenly realize that my skin has somehow changed, become sensitive to the point of being painful to the slightest touch. I'm trundled back to my room and leaned like a sack of wet earth against a body with a voice that tells the other body with a voice, "Pull her leg straight out and put her arm in this hole, will you?" I wonder where my clothes are.

Ten fingers button me down, then loop the brown canvas lifter to my back. I'm transported in what they call the Hoyer lift into the air like a frog in the mouth of a crane. I see clearly out the window to the ground below: trees, a parking lot, a few smokestacks across a river. I must be on the fourth or fifth floor, I think.

Four or five stories up may as well be twenty when you can't move an inch. Still, seeing the cars for a few seconds gives me a moment's reprieve from my pain. However small they look from here, I feel excitement and a sudden burst of hope at knowing even this bit of information. As I land in bed and can no longer see the cars, I remember a day when I was nine and Dad and Mom took me out to the parking lot at Cedarhurst Stadium to teach me how to drive. One hand poised on the wheel, Dad sat beside me, and I felt like a movie star. In the back sat Mom, a worried expression on her face as she inched closer to the door and said, "Watch out for that ditch, Julie!" By the time Dad told me to stop the car and complimented me on my first drive, I had my mind set on taking his motorcycle for a spin.

It was the cycle that had carried Mom and Dad to New York in 1933, and we were never to forget it. Dad kept it under lock and key and took it out for two reasons only: to buy his Johnny Walker Red and to go to the auto-parts store for supplies. It was his prize possession, as everyone in our neighborhood knew.

I don't know why he left the cycle with the key in it that day, but I saw my chance, hopped onto it, turned the ignition, and, on the wings of some miracle, drove onto John Street. Back then I didn't know what trouble was and didn't give a damn about the future. I took off around the block and had no fear of the unknown. I passed the nasty kids on the corner and heard one of the Deluca boys yell, "Go get your dolls and leave the driving to us, little girl!"

After I drove down Mott Avenue, I turned to go back home. As soon as Dad spotted me, he ran toward the motorcycle. I saw fire in his eyes. As I cut the engine, I got scared. The motorcycle slid beneath me. Dad pulled the motorcycle up and kept it from crushing me, so I got only a few cuts on my face, a scrape down my left side, and a really nasty curse from my father.

"I oughta ring your neck, Julie. This thing could fall on you and break your back. Go show your mother what you've done!"

I ran up the front steps, where Joanie grabbed my hand and took me to the mirror. I stared at the scrapes and the blood on my face.

This is the real me, I thought.

. . .

Maybe I've fallen asleep as a beautiful girl and awakened as an old woman without a country or anything to attach herself to but memories that come and go like flies in a room. If someone were to lift me to the mirror on the wall opposite my bed so I could look at myself, would I see the wrinkled face and white hair of an eighty-year-old woman? Bones twisted as if in the final stages of acute arthritis, and my skin, shrivelled and shrunk, containing my whittled body? Would only my eyes reflect my true age?

As I'm lowered into my bed, I realize that I don't know how old I am now. For comfort, I imagine Joanie's hand holding mine. I hear the nurse who gave the orders say, "Glad that's over. She's the worst. Once you get her shower out of the way, the rest of the day's a breeze."

After they leave, I lie in bed trying to remember what happened after I stood at the bottom of the stairs and thought of going up for the aspirin. I remember that my whole body registered the slightest sensation, no matter how minute. I kept hearing my first husband's voice calling me a sex maniac and seeing my old lover's face near the ceiling, as if he were watching me. "Jim's wrong," I said out loud. "I'm not a sex maniac." The sound of my voice startled me, and André's face disappeared into the plaster.

"Honey, come here," George yelled from the living room. "You gotta see this Mets rookie pitch on TV."

Thank God Judy's stopped crying, I thought.

I took the first step up the stairs. Everything appeared

unreal, as if I were underwater watching the world float by. I've got to get two aspirin, I thought, maybe three. Once again, I felt the banister, smooth as marble in my hand. Gilded dust hung in the air. I stumbled on a step, caught myself with the banister. The walls moved toward me, like animals carved in ice. The voices I'd been hearing became faces again, a wall of them surrounding me, cornering me, the way a pack of wolves will close in for the kill. I thought of George.

I mumbled his name and my vision fractured. I saw everything double. I felt a strong beating in my chest and thought I was having a heart attack. My body felt light, like I was going to float to the ceiling and then out into the darkening sky. Everything started to spin. I gripped the banister hard and climbed up the last few steps. Suddenly, I couldn't make out what was in front of me.

I closed my eyes and pulled myself up to the landing. Then I turned left, groping for the wall. I need the aspirin —I'll take some, then go lie down, was all I could think. That's when Judy started to cry again. I froze, not knowing if I should go check on her before I got the aspirin. I decided to feel my way to the bathroom. I took two steps toward the door when my knees gave out. I saw gold glittering around me and felt a spiked ball of sun enter my brain. Then I felt the carpet on my face and puppy fur on my neck, a paw on my cheek. I heard Judy cry and saw a shroud of gray light filtering the gold air. Just before everything went dark, I thought, Baby, stop crying.

• • •

I didn't know what paralysis was until I could move nothing but my eyes. I didn't know what loneliness was until I had to wait all night in the dark, in pain from head to foot, vainly hoping for someone to come with a teardrop of comfort. I didn't know what silence was until the only sound I could make was that of my own breath issuing from a hole drilled into my throat.

Since my memory of the night I passed out came to me, I have lain in bed rehearsing the details again and again, for hours, for months, for years. After I woke up from the coma, I didn't know how much time had passed since my fall on the landing. For many years I didn't know what had happened or where I was. I didn't know when George had found me or if he was taking proper care of Judy. I didn't know how long I could live without knowing where I was or who the strangers were who fed me and changed my diapers and talked about me as if I wasn't there.

No one knows how dark the night is until you can't speak into it.

Chapter Three

HALLELUJAH MARRIAGE

The door to your heart was open
The door to my heart! was open
We went in and
       XXX
We closed the door.
It was dark and you wanted me!
I spoke to Mom and Pop
Hallelujah a courtship.
When the Sabbath day came
Two! hearts stood in front of a priest
We took vows
Made two hearts one
The priest locked the doors
Took a key from his pocket
Drew a rocket
Put the two names on the rocket
With the key to heaven inside
Hallelujah a marriage.

It's the third day after I awoke from the coma. As they're changing my diaper and dressing me, I hear one of the nurses say, "This one's got people coming today. Parents, I think."

The other one says, "Pain in the butt, cuz that means we'll have to clean her up and get Lennox to mop the floors."

My heart misses a beat. I imagine Mother walking in with roses, Father kissing my cheek and telling me everything will be all right. How will I tell them I'm awake? How will I get them to see that I'm aware of everything going on around me? How will I make them understand that I know something horrible has happened but I don't know what?

I stare at the ceiling and the window, now gray with cloud cover, and think, *It might rain, but I'll know their footsteps and their voices. Mother will hold me and tell me how much they miss me, and I'll tell them . . .* I won't *tell* them anything. But I might be able to estimate how long I've been here by any changes in their appearance. I know Mom will see me as alive, awake in a room with no color inside it, a room with no visitors and only one chair. Maybe they're coming to take me home.

Waiting for them, I doze off. Jim, my first husband, is dancing with me the night we met at the Runway Inn. The jukebox plays "Earth Angel (Will You Be Mine)," and Jim's arms wrap around my waist. He takes my chin in his hands and kisses me. His lips feel like home. When he stops kissing me, I pull his face back over mine with my good hands, and I feel his lips again on my capable lips. The song changes to "Only You (and You Alone)" by the Platters, Jim holds me tighter, and . . . I'm touched by the hand of my father.

Dad's wearing his usual dungarees with the grease stains my mom could never wash out, an orange and brown checkered shirt, and a black belt. As he kisses my forehead, I smell cigarette smoke and car grease, and I think of his repair shop back home. His is a man's kiss—strong and rough, tender and soft at the same time. As Dad looks at me, I feel myself floating away again. My first husband's face swims before me, then I remember his dark eyes, his curly black hair, his muscular shoulders.

. . .

I met Jim in the summer of 1955, when I was twenty years old. He was fresh out of the Marine Corps, so I figured my parents would approve. But that wasn't the case—neither Mom nor Dad liked him. Mom told me not to go with someone who was so obsessed with his body that he owned a weight set and worked out every day. Dad conveyed his disapproval by brooding, silently. In one way or another, they both said I'd regret marrying Jim.

Since the spring of 1955, Joanie and I had been sharing an apartment in Far Rockaway, on Beach Thirty-third Street. It was a carefree time when all we had to worry about was paying rent and meeting a husband. Joanie took a job at a clothing shop and I worked at the phone company. Nearly every night after work we'd meet at the Runway Inn for drinks. As the jukebox played the latest rock 'n' roll hits, we'd sip vodka tonics and listen to everything from The Platters to The Fontane Sisters, Fats Domino and LaVern Baker, all the while keeping one eye open for the right man. I believed that the songs we listened to were right, that true love was a magical event cloaked in a nimbus of dream. One day, the songs said, a man would come along, the world would turn right-side up, and all my sadness would disappear.

Movies of the time reinforced this impression of true love. All throughout my teenage years, my girlfriend Peanuts Delgaise and I would go to the Strand Theater on Main Street or to the Gem Theater, where my mother used to go on Friday nights when I was a girl. We'd treat ourselves to giant-screen viewings of the Hollywood stars— Joan Crawford, Lana Turner, Jane Russell, Marlon Brando, Cary Grant, Rock Hudson—we saw them all at seventy-five cents a show. We also went to every Marilyn Monroe picture that came out. I loved the scene in *Gentlemen Prefer Blondes* where Marilyn sang "Diamonds Are a Girl's Best Friend." She quickly became my role model, elevated to the status of a goddess, and her nickname, Blonde Bombshell, didn't scratch the surface of her beauty and sensual power. As a teenager I had vowed to be as attractive as my favorite movie stars Greta Garbo and Zsa-Zsa Gabor, but now with Marilyn making men excited by the mere mention of her name, I had a new screen idol. When I still lived on John

Street, Peanuts and I saw *Niagara* and *How to Marry a Million-aire.* We sat through both pictures twice, and I memorized Marilyn's mannerisms, her clothes, and the way she wore her hair. After I'd moved out of my parents' house and was sharing the Beach Thirty-third Street apartment with my sister, Joanie and I would sometimes joke around. I'd act the part of Marilyn, speaking in a throaty whisper and walking with an exaggerated sway. I even went so far as to bleach my hair blonde, not knowing how dangerous the mixture of peroxide and ammonia was. When Mom saw my new look, she told me that bleaching my hair would make me go bald.

But back then I didn't think about the future. All I wanted was a man who fit the image projected on the golden screen or pressed onto those spinning vinyl discs. So when Jim walked to our table one night at the Runway Inn, I thought I'd found the man I'd been waiting for. Tall and handsome, wearing tight pants and a Marine Corps regula-tion shirt that revealed the toned muscles beneath it, he leaned over our table, gave me a warm smile, and asked me to dance. As we spun around the dance floor, he whispered how beautiful he thought I was and asked if he could kiss me. When I said yes, he held me tightly against him and kissed my mouth in front of everyone.

We dated less than a year before Jim proposed. I can now say that I was physically attracted to him and that I had confused physical union with love. When I said yes to his marriage proposal, I knew only what my parents had taught me and what I'd learned about love in the movies and in pop songs.

Despite my parents' opposition, Jim and I were married in Inwood at Our Lady of Good Counsel Catholic Church on February 12, 1956. It was a few days after my twenty-first birthday and two days before Valentine's Day. I thought the fact of it being a Valentine's wedding would soften my parents' hearts, but my father refused to attend the wedding and my mother came only reluctantly.

After Jim and I were married, Joanie went back home and Jim moved into the apartment on Beach Thirty-third Street. He brought his weights and said I should try using them. He also had a motorcycle he called "Honey." Much to the landlord's chagrin, Honey lived in our kitchen. Jim would polish it and speak to it, as if it were a person. Before long, I realized that Jim was in love with his motorcycle, and not with the woman he'd married. Every once in a while I'd take a potshot and spit on Honey.

Within eight months I was pregnant. Though I knew by this time that something was seriously wrong with my marriage, I continued to indulge in the romantic fantasies portrayed in Hollywood movies and pop love songs. A man named Elvis Presley was all the rage at this time. I first saw his picture in a magazine. He was wearing sunglasses, sitting on a Harley-Davidson motorcycle, smiling that gorgeous smile. His shirt was partly unbuttoned, and I thought I'd never seen such a sexy man. Soon, I watched him on the Ed Sullivan Show and he later dazzled me on the big screen. I heard "Hound Dog" on the radio, but it was "Love Me Tender" that made me, along with all the young girls and the old biddies, swoon. Something in me started to change when I saw Elvis: I realized that my ideal marriage was a dream, that I had confused fantasy with reality, and that Jim and I would never be the perfect couple.

I waited a few weeks before I told Jim that I was pregnant. The day I wanted to quit my job, I made a special dinner for him. I didn't know how he'd react, so I wanted to break the news gently. When I told him, his face froze, his eyes looked fiery, and he started screaming across the table. "No, no, no! I don't want any children! How could you go and do this?"

I felt anger rising in me thick as bile in my throat.

"You know how I've always dreamed of having a lot of children," I spat out.

"You don't deserve kids until you can learn discipline. You don't learn that by being a sex maniac."

I couldn't believe what I was hearing. I grabbed a butcher knife and lunged at him. He moved away from the table, and I held the knife in the air. I stared straight into his eyes, half hating myself, half hating him. It was the first time I'd seen Jim really scared. I went at him and he ducked, caught my arm, and made me drop the knife. If he hadn't been six inches taller and sixty pounds heavier than I was, I probably would have killed him. After this, Jim hid the other knives from me, as well as scissors, can openers, and his pistol. We were no longer on speaking terms.

I took a job and met André, a married Frenchman twenty years my senior. We had an impassioned, imprudent affair that I would now regret, had it not involved the most love and affection I've ever felt from a man. With a rashness that still startles me, we took off one day for California. We'd drive for a few hours, then stop at some bar in the middle of nowhere, then drive to another town and find a place to spend the night. If we both hadn't been married, we'd probably still be there.

But since André had a seven-year-old daughter and I was pregnant, we could only enjoy the moment. I thought at the time that it was pure bliss to live such an unfettered and irresponsible lifestyle, even if it was short-lived. A month later, we returned to Inwood, and I got my old job back at the phone company. I worked day and night until I'd saved enough money to fly to Mexico and divorce Jim.

After that, I thought life would take a turn for the better. But that wasn't the case. One night only a few weeks after I'd returned to work, I lost consciousness and had to be taken by ambulance to Saint Joseph's Hospital. I gave birth to a stillborn baby girl.

. . .

Mother stands beside Dad. She leans over and presses her lips to my forehead. Her dress is printed with green circles. I smell the familiar detergent of our old washroom where I used to do the laundry. Father walks to the foot of my bed, and I start to cry in my silent way.

"Don't cry, Julie. Don't cry, sweet girl," my mother says, as if she thinks I can understand her. "I love you, baby girl. Please wake up. Please, dear God in heaven, wake up."

She leans against me, and as I'm trying to figure out how to ask how Judy is and what's happened to George, Judy steps from behind my mother. She's wearing a thick white coat with black spots and puffy fringes around the sleeves. It must be getting cold out, I think. Mother lifts Judy into her arms, and I can see her small, black shoes, each with a buckled strap across the top. I don't recognize them. She's wearing white socks, and her hair is neatly combed, Shirley Temple style. She's grown. She must be close to two, I guess, which means I've been here for at least eight months. I've turned thirty-two years old since I've been here.

I think of that lost time and make a small sobbing sound, a quiet wailing. I realize that I must have been in the coma for more than six months—long enough for my daughter to need a new pair of shoes. I feel like I'm crying buckets, but hardly any tears come. Judy stares at me, and my mother looks down, saying nothing.

. . .

I had met my husband one evening in Coco's drugstore on Mott Avenue. Though we recognized each other because the house George had grown up in was only a block away from ours, we'd never said more than a passing hello. Whether it was true or not, I'd always thought that he, like the other Italians in our vicinity, would scorn me because of my heritage.

In the drugstore, he surprised me by striking up a conversation. He told me that he was a professional golf instructor. He looked directly into my eyes when he spoke. His look conveyed a sense of trust and concern, along with an obvious physical attraction. Unlike my preconception of him, he didn't show a smidgen of high-mindedness or conceit. After speaking, he looked down at the floor and shuffled his feet like a schoolboy.

Since it was common knowledge that I was an athletic woman, George asked about my hobbies. After the stillbirth of my baby two years before, I'd decided to treat myself better and get into shape. This was the heyday of my sports activities. I told George how I loved to swim the two miles from Roaches Beach to Atlantic Beach and how I also liked to go hunting, ice skating, and horseback riding. I said that I sometimes even fished in Hook Creek. I also told him that my dream was to be the first woman to drive the midget cars at the Indianapolis 500. When I said this, George's mouth dropped open and he smiled.

I still remember thinking how I liked being in his presence. Stout and five years my senior, he had never married. He seemed genuinely interested in me, so when he asked me out on a date, I accepted. When I drove home in my convertible and felt my bleached-blonde hair blowing, I had a feeling that we would marry.

We kept it simple. On November 8, 1963, we took

vows from a justice of the peace in Connecticut. I wore a brown checkered secondhand dress, instead of a white gown. This was fine with me, since I'd already been through one awkward marriage.

We didn't go on a honeymoon. I took this as a slight, even if I had been married before. I thought we should have gone on a short, inexpensive vacation, maybe to a secluded spot somewhere upstate. George thought otherwise. Since I'd had a proper wedding and honeymoon the first time around, he reasoned, I'd have something uncomplicated this time.

We went to George's brother's home in Connecticut, not far from the office of the justice of the peace. Frank and his wife made us a nice spaghetti dinner. We listened to some music, had a little wine, and talked about politics. Though I wasn't very interested in politics, I had taken a shine to John F. Kennedy from the start. I voted for him in the 1960 election, followed the Bay of Pigs invasion of Cuba in 1961, and read about the construction of the Berlin Wall. Through these crises, I'd seen Kennedy as a man of men, a courageous, powerful, levelheaded leader whose liberal views would, I hoped, transform our world into a better place to raise children. And on top of his expertise, John Kennedy was a very sexy man. He was clean-cut and had a smile as appealing as Elvis Presley's and James Dean's. Like many others, I thought Kennedy was a true American hero.

Though Frank and his wife agreed with me, George

was skeptical. He worried that Kennedy was in serious trouble with the Russians. When I countered that the Russians would have attempted to construct missile bases in Cuba if Nixon or anyone besides Kennedy had been president, George listened to me and nodded his head. "Maybe you're right," he said, "but I still think Kennedy's in for trouble." I realized then that, unlike Jim, George could listen to me and accept that I had my own opinions.

George and I headed back to Inwood and began our life together. I worked two days a week at George's brother-in-law's beauty parlor and George gave golf lessons at the Lawrence Country Club. On the afternoon of November 22, 1963, as I was driving home in George's black coupe, I heard the news on the radio: John F. Kennedy had been shot in Dallas. I couldn't believe this had happened only two weeks after we'd been discussing Kennedy over dinner at Frank's. How could someone shoot the president? I wondered as I began to cry. The United States must be going downhill for such an atrocity to happen.

When I got home, George had the TV on. The screen showed Kennedy's black limousine with the president and First Lady inside it, waving to the crowd. Then there was the shot, and I couldn't make out anything but a rushing movement and Jacqueline Kennedy trying to cover her husband's body with hers. I remember that she had blood on her dress, and that her pillbox hat had fallen to the ground. I cried and cried as the crowd learned what had happened and broke into chaos. Besides the president and his wife, I mourned for the couple's children, wondering how they would get by without a father. I wondered what I would do if my husband were killed and we had children that I'd have to raise alone.

The months passed, Lyndon Johnson stepped in as president, and George and I settled into married life. We talked about children of our own, and when I told him that I wanted a large family, he smiled and said he'd like that too. Within nine months of our wedding, I became pregnant with Judy. Throughout the pregnancy I worked at the beauty parlor, fished, drove my car (at half my usual breakneck speed), and swam. I quit drinking. I was afraid that this baby would die, as my first child had, during birth. Even though I didn't consider myself a believer, I wanted a baby so badly that I made a promise to Saint Jude: If the baby was born healthy, I'd name the child, male or female, after him.

Then, just before the due date, without any warning I lost consciousness for the second time. Luckily, George was home and called immediately for an ambulance, which took me to Saint Joseph's Hospital on Far Rockaway. I was kept under heavy sedation while I gave birth on May 26, 1965, to a healthy baby girl.

After we'd returned home from the hospital, George announced that we were moving into my dream house: a vintage 1930s Tudor on Roosevelt Street that I'd imagined owning since I was a girl. It had a brick exterior with a slate roof, a stately fireplace, and gabled doors. An immaculate

lawn of plush green surrounded the house, and beds of mar-
igolds graced the front porch. I'd sometimes look out the
kitchen window and smile in gratitude and awe at owning
this house, remembering how I used to finagle Joanie and
Midge into walking an extra block on our way home from
school just so I could look at it. I loved the heavy wooden
gate opening onto the backyard, the pine trees, and the
brick walk meandering through beds of tulips and shorn
hedges. Sometimes we'd stop long enough to peep through
cracks in the fence. *One day*, I thought, *I'm going to have it.*

And now, by the sweat of George's brow and some
miracle thrown in for good measure, I did have it. Through
the fall of 1966, life was sweeter than it had ever been. I was
elated to be married to the man who'd given me the two
things I valued most—a family and that Tudor house. I
continued washing hair one or two afternoons a week at
my brother-in-law's beauty parlor. Mostly, though, I stayed
home, taking care of Judy and, when the adoption neared
completion, getting to know our two foster children. I re-
decorated the house and arranged the new furniture we
bought for the living room. I went around singing "Chapel
of Love," thinking the world was at my feet.

When George was at work, Judy and I would some-
times sit in the backyard, near one of the majestic pines.
Though she was an infant, I'd tell her the names of things.
I loved to think that each physical object had a different
sound attached to it. Since I'd never completed high school,
I wasn't great at spelling or the proper use of grammar. But

I loved words, the way they sounded, as if a word were an actual reflection of a thing itself.

Language meant music to me. I loved its cadences, its rhythms, its compression and brevity. My mother's broken English was disharmony, obstruction. She took the music from the language and left a half-empty shell of meaning. At an early age, I rebelled against her voice and decided that I'd always be well spoken. On the lawn with Judy, I said "pine" and it sounded as tall and grand as that tree in our yard; "rose" was the sound of mother's love and my own guilt at having betrayed it; "apple" had the taste of sweetness, "radish" of bitterness; "garden" was a land of makebelieve where miracles grew; "mother" was another name for garden. Before Judy was old enough to crawl, she'd heard many of my favorite words.

I'd kiss Judy's ear and whisper "marigold" into it, and in my mind a field of bright orange and yellow flowers appeared before us. She'd put her hands on my face, brushing my chin, touching her fingers to my eyes, giggling in a voice that was as innocent as anything alive and human. "Skin" sounded like the round tips of her soft fingers, and "lips" were what I used to kiss her. "Morning" was faint light, "noon" was the direct summer sun, and "ocean" meant Roaches Beach, a few miles away at Far Rockaway. There we spent many an afternoon, an umbrella arched over us, Judy's face close to mine, her green eyes deep wells I could see down into, her laugh full of joy at seeing and touching me.

. . .

Now, in front of my hospital bed, Judy seems to fear me. "This is your mother," my mom says in her thick Polish accent. "Give her a kiss, Judy."

She puts my daughter down. Judy walks to the bed, leans against the mattress, and hoists herself up with her little arms. But she can't reach high enough, so Mom picks her up and holds her over me. I see an angelic face with big green eyes, thick auburn hair, clear skin, and bright, shiny baby teeth. Judy kisses me reluctantly, tentatively, a quick peck placed shyly on my cheek. The kiss doesn't make a sound. Her eyes close tightly, as if she's afraid of me, and she uses my chest to push herself away. I think, *This is the first kiss I've ever received from her*, because she was just fourteen months old when I collapsed that night on the landing. I love her eyes up close, her little nose and smart expression. She looks spoiled, I think. But then I see fear in her eyes. She's afraid of coming too close to me. If Judy's this scared, I must look horrifying. But since I've not yet seen myself, I don't know what's scaring her.

Mom puts Judy back down on the floor, where she stands facing me, looking like she doesn't know what to do next. Mom turns away, and I see her shoulders shaking and hear her breath coming in broken gasps. Tears streaming down his face, Father stands at the foot of the bed. *I've never seen him cry*, I think. As he hits the wall, I feel a frustrated sorrow I'd not thought possible.

That's what I want to do: hit a wall, or a person, or God. Mom says something to him about calming down.

I am now terrified. They both must think there's no hope. Their anguish and my daughter's fear of me are harder to take than the pain in my arms and legs, than my inability to tell them that I'm alive. I try to indicate that I'm cognitive by raising my head an inch off the pillow and moving it from side to side. I also move my eyes toward them, then up to the ceiling, then down toward the floor. Either they don't notice or they think it's an ordinary movement I make, a gesture devoid of meaning.

Judy stands to the left of my bed, staring at me. Mom repeats, "That's your mother, Judy," and the pain of these words tears my heart in two. Who would want a mute, disfigured person for a mother, someone who can't embrace her child? As I acknowledge this pain, I feel a rage that hits me in the gut. I want to scream at them and at what's happened to me. How could I have gone from a woman who attracted men wherever she went to someone people now looked on as subhuman? Did I cause this? Was there no hope of returning to my normal self?

The three of them stand this way for a few awkward minutes while frustration tears me apart. I lean my head back and feel every disfigured bone in my body fill with rage. Mother's shoulders stop shaking, but Father continues to cry until he says, "I can't take it anymore." He goes out of the room, his shoulders slumped, the sound of his crying still audible.

Judy is quiet. After Father leaves, Mom sits in the chair across from my bed and stares at me. Judy crawls into Mom's lap and fiddles with the straps of her purse. The more Mom looks at me, the more uncomfortable I feel. What does she want from me? Why is she staring at me? I hear her say, "Julie . . . Julie," in the tone she used when I did something wrong. "Oh, Julie," she repeats, and I realize how much pain I've caused.

. . .

One day when I was in fourth grade, I was playing by the Skpansky's oak tree. I could hear Mrs. Skpansky blasting Beethoven's Fifth Symphony from her living room. Even though Dad called this "Communist music," I loved the loud drums and cymbals. I swung from a branch and landed on the ground as two of the mean boys on our block were walking down Wahl Avenue. As they passed the Skpansky's drive, one of them pointed at the Anderson's house.

"Yeah, they're a bunch a niggers."

I stared at the boys as they passed and thought about that word.

That day, after lunch, when I was helping do the dishes, I asked, "Mom, why is Mrs. Anderson a nigger?" She stopped rinsing suds and took the towel from the counter. I knew by the way she moved it slowly over her skin that I'd said something wrong.

She stared at me for a long moment, then said, "Julie, where did you learn that word?"

"From the fifth-graders."

"Do you know what it means?" she asked in her clumsy accent.

"Yes. It means Mrs. Anderson and Buddy and Jason and Mame."

By then Mom was standing over me. I got scared and thought I'd said something wrong.

"Julie, you don't have the right to call someone such an ugly name. To make you remember how bad is that word, I'm going to get the hairbrush." Whenever she wanted to discipline us, Mom got out the big blue brush with the wiry bristles.

I started to go toward the side door, so I could run into Dad's shop. He'd make Mom stop. As soon as Mom saw me dart for the door, she grabbed me by the hair, dragged me over to the kitchen table, pulled out a chair, and forced me to sit down.

"You stay right there until I get back. You move one muscle and you're not leaving this house for a week."

I heard her go upstairs to the bathroom. With each step back down the staircase, she became more of a monster. When she came into the kitchen, I closed my eyes and felt the hard, smooth back of the brush strike my shoulder and head. I felt the bristles and I opened my eyes. Mother was furious. She held me by the hair and yelled, "Look at me! Are you ever going to say that bad word again, Julie?"

I thought of Mom calling Dad "Gypsy Horwat" and Dad calling Mom a "Nazi Pollack." I was angry enough to hit her back. If I had been an inch taller or a month older, I would have, I swear. I looked up into her eyes, saw them burning, felt my own eyes stinging and my heart beating. I refused to answer her question.

"Oh, I see, little Julie, you want to fight your big fat mother? You be sorry, I promise."

With her hand pulling my hair, she dragged me to the sink. I didn't scream or show any pain. I watched her put the brush on the counter, then reach for a bar of soap. "If you don't say you're sorry this instant, I'm going to wash your mouth out, and I don't mean maybe. Do you know what soap tastes like?"

I looked at her holding out that white bar and felt such hatred that I couldn't speak.

"You're going to apologize?" She looked at me.

I looked straight back. She turned on the water and pushed the soap close to my mouth. It had a dark spot on it. Water dripped from her hand onto the sink and my red checkered dress. Still, I didn't say anything.

"Okay, Julie. You're getting too big for your britches."

She put the soap against my lips. I felt its texture, smooth as marble. "Say you're sorry."

I remained silent.

Her hand pulled me so close to her that I felt the soft female flesh. She let go of my hair and tried to open my mouth. I clamped my jaw shut. She became so furious her eyes seemed to glow.

"You're going to regret this. I'll show you a thing or

two." She yanked me by the hair and took me out into the yard. She led me to some dog feces and pushed my face close to it. I started screaming as loudly as I could. Dad ran out of his shop at the same moment that Mrs. Anderson's sister, Mame, came barreling around the corner of our house.

"What's goin' on here?" my father asked. "I can hear you all the way down the block, Mary. Let go of her!"

"She called Mrs. Anderson 'nigger,' " my mother said, looking askance at Mame. "At her age, Joe!"

By then I couldn't hear a word she said. I leaned my head against my father's stomach and smelled the tobacco odor of him. As he rubbed my hair, Mame rested her hand on my shoulder and looked at my mother. "Mary," she said, "there's too much wickedness in this world. She's just a child. She'll learn."

. . .

"Julie. Oh, Julie."

Mother stares at me for a long while. Then, as if mumbling to herself, she says, "That husband of yours! I don't know what I'm going to do with him!"

I look straight at her, grateful for any news about George.

"After he told us you shook him awake that night and couldn't move your left side, that poor man, like a baby he cried. Been cryin' ever since. He told us that the ambulance came and took you to Saint Joseph's. You weren't awake anymore. But I was there when you woke up, Julie. I was there when you talked. Clear as day, you cried and said, 'What's going to happen to me? Who's going to take care of my baby?'"

The last thing I recall thinking is, *Baby, stop crying.* I don't remember anything after I passed out. I have no recollection of being in any hospital or of hearing anyone speaking to me or of being able to speak myself.

"Your father and me was there at the hospital. We could hear you screaming all the way down the hall. Jezus Chrystus! Joanie was there, too. You kept yelling, 'I don't know what's wrong with me, Joanie. Please take care of my baby.'"

Mom pulls a handkerchief from her bag. Why does she keep talking, I wonder, if she thinks I don't understand her?

She wipes her eyes and touches Judy's hair. "That was right after the doctors said you could go home as soon as your body had stabilized. That's when the second one came. What's the word?" She looks into my eyes. "Oh, yes. Hemorrhage. That's it. That one almost killed you, my sweet girl. On top of that, George told Joanie that he wanted his sister Mae to raise the baby."

I look at Judy and can see that she's being taken care of. Just so she's fed and properly clothed, I won't worry. And as long as I can see how beautiful she is, I won't miss her so much.

She reaches up and starts playing with the collar of mother's dress.

"But how could George just leave you lying here? And this little one," she continues, looking down at Judy, "how could he move back with his sisters instead of letting Joanie take her?"

She says some words in Polish then, and I get the gist of their meaning. What I wouldn't give to cuss now.

She lifts Judy off her lap and approaches the bed. Slowly, she turns my head and begins stroking my hair. My throat hurts where the tube pierces it, and I make a groaning sound.

Father walks back in, his cheeks still wet. He bends down again to kiss me. He caresses my forehead. Once more, I smell cigarettes and the car grease in his stained clothes.

"We'll be back, Julie," he says.

Mom starts to cry. "We'd better go," she says. "Kiss your mother good-bye, Judy." She lifts my daughter in her arms, and Judy kisses me one more time on the cheek.

I turn my head to see the three of them walk out, Judy between them, holding their hands. The last thing I see is her thick white coat with the black spots on it. It must be wintertime.

Chapter Four

BREATHING

I lie flat on my back in bed.
For God's sake, let my next breath be it.
I used to race cars,
cycles, boats,
skis and skates,
fish and hunt
I ask God—
Let my next breath be my last.

My parents made a few more visits without Judy before I came down with my first bout of pneumonia. My lungs filled with fluid, and the hole in my throat became walled in mucus. The oxygen seemed to have been siphoned from the room, and I felt like I was suffocating. Hour by hour, the simple act of breathing required more effort. My body ached, my joints throbbed as if consumed by fire, and my temperature rose. My body felt swollen and engorged. I began to confuse reality with dream—my life before what my mother called the hemorrhage and my new one, paralyzed.

I slept and dreamed. Jim and I lie on a beach. White sand stretches for miles. I'm wearing a gold strapless bathing suit. Jim's red swimming trunks stretch tight around his waist, and his chest hairs lie slicked down with sweat. On his right arm, the tattoo of a black panther is sprinkled with sand. The sea shines turquoise blue, and no matter how far we swim out, I can see the sand on the ocean floor. Jim pulls me close to him in the water. His hands touch my back and neck, my wet hair. His lips taste of salt. As I wrap my legs around his waist, he lifts me into the air. The sun gleams on his hair, making each strand shine. He lowers me back into the water and slides my suit off my shoulders. His trunks float away. I lean close to him and whisper, *I want to have your child*. He smiles and pulls me to the shore, kissing me on the mouth and throat. But there's a commotion and I wake up to someone lifting me onto a gurney.

"Her fever's been rising for two days," I heard a voice say. "She's coming down with something. Head nurse wants her transferred off this ward."

I was lifted in the Hoyer, then lowered onto the gurney by hands that seemed attached to nothing but air.

"C-41," a male voice said.

I tried to remain awake, but my eyes grew heavy. I dozed. When I woke up, I was being lifted from the gurney onto another bed. I heard a familiar voice, as if Joanie was calling from far away. I thought I was dreaming, until her voice became louder and I slowly realized that she was standing beside my bed. I opened my eyes and saw my sister.

Joan! The person who most closely resembled what I looked like before my body malfunctioned, the person who knew me better than anyone else. She was wearing a tan hat, and her hair, longer than I'd remembered, was combed back and tied in a cropped ponytail. Her skin was pale and flawless.

She carried a potted plant in her hands. The plant had red flowers, and as Joan bent down closer to me, I saw it was a geranium. Though tears formed in the corners of her eyes, my sister smiled. She placed her lips to my forehead in the first gesture of physical comfort since my daughter had kissed me a few weeks before.

"Hi, Julie. I know you're hearing everything. I can tell by the expression on your face that you're alive and conscious and thinking."

She looked into my eyes for a moment, and I thought of the picture I'd seen as a girl of a blue-robed Mother Mary holding the bleeding Jesus. I wanted to be held. But for that to happen I'd have to be turned toward her, and she'd have to put her arms around the front of me and wrap them around what was left of my girth.

She didn't hold me. She went to the sill and put the plant there, where the sun could strike it in the late afternoons. As her arm extended to put the pot down, I saw how my own arm used to look, lean and feminine, strong and shapely at the same time, vibrant and fully alive.

She came and sat next to where I lay half reclined, half raised to a sitting position. She smelled of Jean Naté. We sat in silence for a moment. Normally, in the old days before I married Jim, we'd have already been gossiping about men or imitating Tallulah Bankhead and Bette Davis or planning to meet after work at the Runway Inn for a vodka collins. If I couldn't join her because I had a date, we'd talk about Midge's new boyfriend or the jealousy we felt toward our brother, Joey, for being Mom's pride and joy.

Instead, we sat in silence until Joanie said, "I know you can hear everything I'm saying, cuz I was in the hospital that first awful night when you could still speak. You kept saying, 'I'm sick, Joanie. Please take care of my baby.' I cried and prayed and touched your left arm, which was already paralyzed."

She touched my arm when she said this. She got up and went to the geranium in the window. A soft light had already begun to shine on it. I turned my neck an inch or two and was able to see my sister's fingers pluck a sere leaf out of the petals.

Joan said, "Mom and Dad send their love. They're doing fine, just fine, except Mom's eyes are bothering her. She's started taking Epogen, cuz the anemia's getting worse. Judy is fine, too—growing like a weed. Sad thing is that George had to sell the house."

I felt woozy. The light in the room became gray. In my mind's eye, someone pulled the plug and my dream house went down the drain. My sister's voice sounded like it was getting farther away from me. I remembered how I used to paint her fingernails all shades of red and orange. I thought about the first time Mrs. Anderson gave us pancake makeup and how Joan and I went upstairs and stood in front of the mirror and fixed each other's hair up in a sweep. We put that makeup on and felt like real ladies and went downstairs, then out onto the front porch and stood, thinking someone would come by and tell us how beautiful we looked. As luck would have it, Joey came running around the corner. Joanie yelled, "Look at us, Joey! Me and Julie are grown-up ladies now, cuz Mrs. Anderson gave us makeup." Joey came real close to us, looked at our faces and hair, then ran into Dad's garage. In less than a minute, Dad came out and stomped onto the porch and grabbed my chin and said, "What are you, a couple of *putta?*" He looked me right in the eye when he said it, then turned to Joan and said, "Both of you—go in the house this instant and get that junk off your face before I dunk you in a grease pan." We ran into the house, past our mother, who could do nothing to help us, up the stairs and into the bathroom, where we washed the makeup off our faces, crying all the while.

Still talking, Joan turned from fingering the geranium leaves. I hadn't heard a word she'd said. She pinched a leaf between thumb and forefinger. "Mae is taking care of Judy when George goes to work at the club, and I'll back you six ways from Sunday she's telling that child rotten things about her mother."

I was too fatigued to feel angry. I looked at Joan's

lanky body by the window, her shoulder blades beneath her wool dress. She took off her hat and placed it on the radiator. *If she leaves it there*, I thought, *it might catch fire and all my troubles will be over.* She turned and looked me straight in the eye, as if she knew what I'd just been thinking. She walked back to the bed and touched her hands to my forehead.

"You're warm, Julie. I hope they took your temperature."

I looked up at her and could not tell her that each breath was difficult. I had begun to ache all over.

"When they had you in that ice, I knew you'd never be the same."

What ice? I thought. She read my face.

"You were packed in that ice, first at Saint Joseph's for two weeks, then in the ambulance, in this special ice thing. At Mount Sinai, you were laid in sheets filled with liquid nitrogen, which is colder than ice. No one, not even family, could talk to you. Mother cried all the time, and Father was riled and feeling helpless. You know what happens when he feels helpless."

She paused, got a faraway look in her eyes, and glanced at the window, then back at me.

"I thought you'd never be conscious again. But I know you are. I can see it in your eyes. Ten to one you're hearing everything I say."

A tear formed in the corner of my right eye, and as I felt its sting, I knew Joanie would see it. But she went back to the geranium and didn't see that tear fall.

"Crimony, Julie, that ice scared me—you all packed up in the ambulance on the way to Mount Sinai; and once we were there, George rushing in from the golf club; and me screaming, 'I'm *not* getting out of the room! She's *my* sister, for Christ's sake!'—it all scared the living daylights out of me."

She came back from the plant and bent down over me. I saw tears well up in her eyes and spill over in the luxury of a human being alive and able to express her emotions. She looked straight at me, so close that I could see how her eyes had specks of sea green in the iris.

"Back in that emergency room, I knew you were alive, so I told you the dirtiest jokes I could think of. I could even see your expression change at the punch lines. Not a smile, mind you, but a change nonetheless. Kind of a raising of your upper lip. But they kept telling me your brain waves had stopped, or some damn thing."

My tears fell then. Joan saw them and became silent. She touched my face and raised her index finger to my cheekbone. Sitting on the bed, she remained silent, and I thought, *Who, if I cried, would see me?* And I knew it would be my tomboy sister.

"Julie, I love you. I know you can hear me, and I want you to realize how much I love you and how much we all miss your company. It's been real hard to visit as often as we'd like. What, between Midge getting married and moving to Texas and me raising the children. But after they brought you here, Mom and I used to make the trip every second to third week. Once in a while, we'd move your arms, Mom on one side, me on the other."

She wiped a tear from her cheek. She got up, went to the door, and called for a nurse. The nurse came into the room and approached Joan with a smile she never used on me. Joanie said, "My sister hears everything I'm saying. She's alive! I'm telling you, she understands what's going on around her."

The nurse stood in white, statuesque as marble. I watched as she smiled and didn't say a word. Joan stood beside her and looked like she was going to beat the nurse up. The nurse looked down at me in a false expression of pity, then turned to Joan, touched her on the arm, and said, "I'm sorry, Ma'am. The doctors have determined that your sister isn't cognitive of her surroundings."

"Listen, you idiot, don't tell me what my sister is or isn't capable of. Don't tell me who she is or isn't, or if she sees or knows or hears, or what the goddamned doctors tell you. I know her like the back of my own damned hand, and I'm telling you she's aware of what's going on in this room right now. She just cried. She knows. She can hear us!"

"Ma'am, I know how difficult this must be for you. We deal with these situations every day. But try to understand. Truth is, your sister's had two massive strokes. Strokes destroy a person's motor abilities, sometimes cognitive functions, too. Blood flow to the brain is interrupted, and the person loses consciousness, like your sister did."

Joan looked like she was going to smash the room to

pieces. I smiled inside as she started screaming profanities.

"Please calm down before I call security," the nurse threatened.

"Go ahead," Joan screamed, "get your damned security, for all I care. My sister's my best friend. She's sick, but she knows what's going on, I'm telling you."

The nurse walked calmly out the door.

I thought of that word *stroke*, and the room began to spin. Those six letters crowded out my thoughts, tumbled and rolled me in a wave I couldn't swim out of, and just as the wave curled, I was dragged under. My lungs felt like they were filling with fluid. I saw Joan's face floating beside me, her lips forming that new word, *stroke*. Just before everything went black, Joan held my face between her palms and looked me in the eye.

"Come what may, I know you're alive down there. No matter what, come hell or high water, I'm going to get you out."

. . .

When I woke up, a nurse was checking an IV that hung by my bed. The room was quiet. My mouth was as dry as on the day I woke up from the coma and my lungs felt like they were on fire. Sun pooled along the radiator and around my bed rails, creating eddies of shadow and light around the potted plant Joan had given me. Yellow fire on the bright red flowers, the undersides of the leaves in darkness, the pot the color of Arizona earth I drove across that long-ago trip with André. We stopped at a lake and walked down to the water. André kissed me. His lips felt soft as baby powder. I thought of my father's whiskers and the way he'd stand at the bathroom sink most mornings and apply the lather and the Old Spice that would always smell like men to me.

Who, I thought, will water the plant? Who will go on sturdy legs to the sink and turn the spigot and fill a cup and walk to the window?

No matter if Joanie is in the room or not, her fingers will part those leaves forever. Hope had my sister's face, her hands fluttering mad as birds around the nurse. Hope had my sister's anger filling the room with the accusations I would have spoken if I had had my voice back, if I had had a tongue normally hinged and a mouth that would form around words.

Each day I thought I'd be wheeled into the corridor lined with bright ceiling lights. Each day I thought would be the last I'd have to stare at those white walls that became, in my fever, pink as the roses in my mother's garden, green as my daughter's eyes, red as Joanie's anger. Each day I expected to be taken away.

One day I was. I felt my body being raised into the air, then lowered onto a gurney.

"That crazy sister of hers thinks she's conscious," said one nurse to another as she forced my legs together. "Day before yesterday she starts yelling at me, and I had to get security after her. But what do you expect when you lose someone close to you? Now, she's got pneumonia and has to be taken to Bellevue. You think her sister's going to blame me for that, too?"

Before the other nurse could answer, two men came into the room. They wheeled me down the corridor, away from respirators and difficult breathing, away from the light falling in puddles around the window shade, the sill, my forgotten geranium.

Chapter Five

DEATH I

Hallelujah! Hallelujah,
I have stopped breathing.
My eyes are shut but I can see!
My mind is functioning
yet no one can talk with me.
All the same, I lie here so comfortably.

Look at the weeping people.
Boy, are they crying up a storm.
Look at poor Mom's eyes.
It just shows I'm part of Mom gone.

There goes the jealous one
I beat up once for kissing my boyfriend.
She looks mighty happy. Oh, well.
I guess I'll go to hell.

Death, death, death.
The hardest part
is getting my soul into an unborn.

I'm wheeled out of room C-41 and into a hall. People sit silently in wheelchairs or lie atop gurneys. The fever makes me delirious. I can focus my eyes for only a few seconds at a time before the hallway becomes enveloped in fog. I see a legless man whose skin is as dark as the earth Mother used to water beneath her rosebushes. As the men wheel me past, I smell cigarette smoke and see that the man's torso ends at his thighs. A sheet lies flat where his legs should be. My vision blurs, and his face melts into the sheets until only his eyeballs lie on the gurney, staring up at me.

I try to scream, but my lips are thick and heavy. I am taken down in an elevator, then wheeled along a dark corridor. Neither of the men says what Bellevue is or how I'm going to get there. At the end of the corridor is a door. A blinding light strikes my face, and I see an ambulance.

I am lifted into it. The light is so bright I think I'll go blind. I shiver because of the cold. Someone drapes a sheet over me, the door slams, and an oxygen mask is placed like a hand over my face. I want that hand to smother me. Instead, it helps me breathe.

The engine starts and my eyes close.

When I woke up, I was hoisted into a burning light so cold that I could see the men's breath as they carried me into a door marked Emergency. I was wheeled into a room and laid in a bed. Someone rolled me over and slid a thermometer into my rectum, the way Dr. Oliver used to take Judy's temperature when she was a baby.

"A hundred and two," a male voice said. "Let's get her on antibiotics immediately. And lung suction through the trach every hour."

My face felt bloated. I wanted someone to pour cold water over me. Alien hands turned me onto my back; a needle was poked into my skin. I started to drowse, and a hand came into view, holding a syringe with no needle. The hand pried my jaw open and slipped the tip of the syringe into my mouth. I tasted a thick, bitter liquid. I gagged and felt some of the liquid spew out the tube in my throat, onto my chest. An unfamiliar female voice said the first kind words from any hospital member since I had awakened from the coma.

"There, now. Let's just hope you're going to be okay."

Far from being okay, I learned later that I almost died from this bout of pneumonia. I don't have a clear sense of how it happened, but one minute I was listening to the nurse's soothing voice, and the next I was being stuck in the arms with more needles.

The nurse whose voice made me drift off to sleep stood next to the bed. She must have been leaning down to me, because I heard her voice as if it were inside my head.

"Just hold on," she kept saying. "Hold on to your life."

I didn't want to hold on. I wanted to drift away and never return to my broken body, my desecrated life. I wanted to go back to sleep and sink down to the warmth of death. I was almost there when someone started beating my chest while someone else yelled, "One! Two! Three!" Each time he got to three, someone's hand struck my chest. I tried to will myself under, to go unconscious. Nothing hurt, and everything hurt. The man wouldn't stop pounding my chest.

I opened my eyes and saw two doctors hovering over me. Three or four nurses scurried into the room. I saw everything around me but felt nothing. I was able to look down at the scene: I saw myself lying on that bed. I actually *saw* the fever moving through my body and my emaciated chest beneath the doctor's hands. I saw the blood flowing in my vessels. I saw my closed eyes. I heard the sound of my own breath diminishing, and I knew I was dying. Knowing this made me happy.

The doctor stopped pumping my chest and took a clear plastic bag from a nurse. Inside the bag was a pump, a face mask, and a coil of clear plastic tubing. I watched the doctor place the mask over my face. I did not move when he put the mask over my mouth and nose. Watching this, I was calm. The part of me above the room wanted this to be happening. I liked the drama of it.

This went on for about an hour. The part of me above the room became impatient for my body to let go. I kept telling her to take off the mask, to roll her head to the side when the doctors went out of the room. I watched her attempt to jimmy the mask from her face, managing to knock it askew. The part of me hovering cheered. But someone's hand always put the mask back on. *Why won't they stop? Why won't they let her die?* I thought.

The bright light in the room transformed into a foggy haze. *This is the in-between world*, I thought. At that moment, I saw my grandmother, long since dead, floating in the air beside me, and beyond her a riverbank. She was wearing a purple dress with little white flowers on it, a purple cloth belt, and her black "Granny shoes." Her right hand extended out over the water, while her left clutched her black pocketbook. I was up to my chin in water, listening as she called in a musical voice, "Come to me. Don't be afraid, my child. Come to me." Her voice didn't sound like it had when she was alive; its pitch was higher, as if she were singing. Her face was calm, and she smiled with her beautiful blue-gray eyes. Even though the wind was blowing, her white hair lay unruffled on her head.

Though I didn't say anything, I could tell she understood that I wanted to die. But each time I reached for her hand, the river's current carried me away. The closer I got to the riverbank, the deeper the water became. I tried to swim against the current, but I slipped on wet rocks and the bank of mud before me. I fell. Nana kept getting farther away. "Don't leave me," I screamed, "I want to come with you. Please don't leave me, Nana!"

Then I couldn't feel the river anymore, or the water rushing against my body. I couldn't right myself on the stones beneath my feet. My mind became fuzzy. I thought I was going to drown. At the last second, I realized that I didn't wish to die after all. I didn't want to be laid in a coffin like the one Grandma was put in the day Mom dressed Joanie and me in black and sent us with Dad to Uncle Louie's and Aunt Margaret's in Uniontown and we saw Grandma in that coffin covered in ugly flowers. We paid last respects to the woman who had given birth in a Gypsy wagon to fourteen children and who had tried to teach me the Rosary.

"Come," she said again, "don't be afraid, Julie."

She repeated this three times. Each time, her voice became fainter, harder to hear over the sound of the water pulling me away.

"Come, child. Say the Lord's Prayer with me."

"But Nana," I yelled, "You know I believe in reincarnation."

As I shouted this, Nana disappeared. I thought I was going to drown, but I heard a bell. As the bell clanged, I felt my body being pulled into bed against my will. The part of me watching from above faded away. I screamed until the doctors gave me another shot, and I fell into a drugged sleep.

When I woke up the next day, I didn't know where I was. I even forgot that I'd been taken somewhere in an ambulance. A mask still covered my mouth and nose. I felt more trapped than ever. But I was breathing better, and as soon as my eyes opened, a nurse came into view. She smiled, as if she was happy to see me. She even spoke to me. "I know you can't understand, but rest assured—you're in good hands."

No alarms screamed, and my usual clothes had been replaced by a different cotton gown.

"Thought for a while you were going to leave us," the nurse continued, checking a tube that ran out of my nose and up over my left shoulder. She held a clipboard in her arms and wrote something down. Despite myself, I was grateful for her concern.

"All this racket must be awful for you. And to not know who's taking care of you, right? Well, for the record, I'm Adrienne."

Even though she thought I couldn't understand her, she talked to me normally and hummed softly while she gave me a sponge bath. I was reminded of my father humming to himself while he worked in his shop. Even when she changed my diaper, then removed the mask from my face and slipped the tube from my throat, she touched me with a gentleness that shocked me.

She went to the sink across the room. I heard the sound of running water. When she came back, she held the plastic tube in the air.

"See, all clean. That way, no little critters can get in and give you new infections."

She inserted the tube back into my throat. I smelled rubbing alcohol on her gloves. After she positioned the tube, she unrolled the gloves and pulled the covers snug around me.

"You get some rest now, you hear. Be back later in the afternoon."

. . .

The next day, a doctor came to check on me. The whole time he was in the room, he looked as though he didn't know how to treat someone whose brain he believed was as useless as a rotten eggplant. I wanted to speak with him, to find out when this nightmare would be over. I wanted to know when I'd be well enough to go home and if I'd ever be able to walk and talk again. Yet something in me knew that the answer was *never*.

I couldn't ask anything, and no one volunteered any information. The doctor simply checked a chart and stared straight at me. He didn't touch me. He turned to a nurse.

"We should release her as soon as the lungs clear—two, three days, maximum. At that time, she can be returned to Goldwater."

Never mind that he spoke about me as if I were a book overdue at the library. I kept hearing the word *Goldwater* and wondering what it meant.

Chapter Six

SILENT PRAYER

Past   present   future
Is yesterday   today   tomorrow
Are came   coming
For fire   wind   waves
Question why in threes
In the name of the Father
The Son and the Holy Ghost
Amen.

Three days later, Adrienne removed the oxygen mask and dressed me in the old sky-blue uniform. She called another nurse, and the two of them hoisted me onto a gurney. I lay flat while someone's hands strapped my legs to a metal spur. From somewhere above my head, Adrienne said, "You're going home now."

I have no home, I thought, all the while knowing that she meant the place the doctor called "Goldwater."

"You're a real trooper," she continued. "You fought

off a case of pneumonia that would kill most people in your condition."

Something in me smiled, the way I used to when someone gave me a compliment. I felt my body wheeled down a brightly lit hallway, through open doors and out into a white light that made my eyes burn.

I was lifted into the air and placed in the ambulance on runners that held me steady. I saw a small window in one corner of the car. I turned my head toward it, rolling my eyes to get a good view.

Objects moved past—part of a brick building, the tops of a few bare trees. Then we were on a busy street, emergency siren screaming. Though I couldn't see any road signs, I was sure we were in Manhattan, given the close proximity of high buildings and the slow traffic and car horns blaring. We passed a bridge, and I saw a body of water. We crossed the bridge, the road narrowed, and through my window, I glimpsed flashes of grass along the sides of the river. I saw a fence and gulls perching on it. As the ambulance slowed, I saw parts of another brick building.

We stopped, and I was carried into a building someone called "administration." They put me on a gurney while a woman stood to my right, holding a blue folder. They discussed where I should be taken.

I was wheeled down a hallway, then into an elevator.

When the elevator door opened, I saw a woman sitting in a wheelchair, making the sign of the cross over and over. A blonde woman with neatly painted red lipstick sat close to her, staring out a window. A dark-skinned man sat slumped in his chair; as we passed, he pointed at me and bent his index finger back and forth, beckoning.

Since I'd been in a state of delirium when I was taken out of here, all of this was new to me. Just knowing the name of this place gave me leverage. Information was power, and I wanted more of it. But how was I to get it? How was I to find out my prognosis? Why wasn't anyone in my family here to help me? How long until Joanie would get me out of here? Would I ever be able to speak or sit in a wheelchair like the people crowded in the corridor? I heard voices in conversation. I vowed to listen to each sound around me, to soak in the information. The more information I pieced together, the more I wanted.

I expected to be sent back to the room I had been in when I woke up from the coma. But as I was wheeled down another corridor, I knew this would not be the case. We stopped at an unfamiliar ward. "Here we are," a male voice said from behind me, "D-II." I was wheeled through a set of double doors into a world of quiet.

Silence was a pall over the room, the absence of life. I was afraid that even the meager comforts I had before the pneumonia, such as my window and a few familiar faces, would now be gone. I longed for anything familiar—my window of sky, even alarms going off and nurses cussing—and as I was lifted off the gurney and placed in a bed I'd never lain in before, I looked up to where my window was supposed to be. It was gone. A flaking piece of plaster had taken its place. There was an oblong window to my left, but I couldn't move my head enough to see out of it.

A nurse I'd never seen entered the room. Silently, she hooked a plastic bag onto a metal frame behind me. She moved to the end of the bed, reached down, and cranked the bed up, causing my back to pinch in pain. I grew afraid. Then I realized that I'd be able to see the whole room this way, so I endured the pain in hopes of seeing what was going on around me. Because I was sitting up for the first time, a coughing fit attacked my lungs. Mucus and saliva spewed from my mouth and the tube in my throat. The nurse groaned and said under her breath, "Why'd they send this dead weight to godforsaken Goldwater?"

My arms trembled against my chest. My bones shifted, as if my emotions were directly connected to my skeleton. My fists tightened noticeably, my chest heaved, and I heard a sound—half moan, half snarl—come from my throat. The nurse looked at me for a few seconds, shrugged her shoulders, and walked away, perplexed.

From this sitting position, I saw the room clearly. I could make out the people asleep, some with machines beside them. I wasn't here an hour before the woman in the bed across from me began to writhe uncontrollably. She shook so much that she fell out of bed. A nurse came in, wrestled her back into bed, and put something like an ice-cream stick into her mouth. A second nurse arrived, and the two of them held her down against the mattress. In a moment, the sedated woman became limp and calm.

For a while there was silence. Then the woman whose bed was near the door began to cry. Her mouth hinged open, so I saw how the inside was bright red. Her skin was the color of ash with a tinge of green. She rolled her head to one side and began moaning for a nurse. No one came. She wailed. I listened to the sound, which reminded me of an injured animal, shot but still alive, wishing perhaps to die and be relieved of its misery. She turned in the bed and looked my way, but without any awareness of me showing in her eyes. For hours she lay in that position and cried.

Occasionally, I heard the rustle of bedclothes and the sound of a respirator breathing for the body in the bed catercorner from mine. From the outer corridor, I heard a voice projected from far away, as if it issued from deep inside a dark tunnel.

My body was a ghost, a remembrance of movement once easy, now impossible. I was made of useless bones wrapped in a paper-thin skin that did nothing but feel pain, tempered with rare moments of pleasure, such as when heat blew down over me on a winter day.

Four beds and a mirror, feeding machines, respirators, sky-blue gowns, white sheets, the odor of feces, a white light from above. These were all I knew of my new home.

As darkness fell that first night on the D ward, two nurses made their rounds from bed to bed, readying us for sleep. The one who took care of me stuck a needle in my arm, and I felt a burning sensation.

"Yep, Dillard," I heard the nurse say, withdrawing the needle, "my brother and uncle were drafted. Brother's leaving next week. Crazy white man's war we got to fight makes me sick. Just yesterday, you see it? The man who lit hisself on fire? Jesus, Mary, and all the rest! And this here President Nixon tells us it'll be over and done with by September. Yes, ma'am, by September, year of our Lord, 1969." She started crying then, and the other nurse, the one called Dillard, hugged her and said, "Now you stop your worry. Your brother's gonna be just fine, you wait and see. All anyone has, honey, is hope. Wait and see."

I remembered that I'd voted against Nixon in the election of 1960, and as the two women embraced, I thought, What a miracle to wrap your arms around another person! What a miracle to receive someone else's arms around your body and to feel those arms fold around you, snug as a new winter coat, arms that bolster your courage in the face of the unknown.

And those remarkable words: *nineteen sixty-nine, nineteen hundred and sixty-nine*—a year, a grounding, a lifeline connecting the outside world to room D-11! War and a flash of memory of my little brother couldn't keep out my happiness at knowing which year it was. Nothing could touch the strength I felt in knowing that it was 1969 and that the country was at war, though with whom I had no idea. I was thirty-four. It had been three years since I'd passed out on the gold carpet and nearly two since I'd woken up from the coma. In all that time, my mother and Joan had visited a dozen and a half times. My father had come less frequently. Midge had moved to Texas, and Joey had never come. I hadn't seen any of my friends I used to work with, or the girls Joanie and I used to meet with for drinks at the Runway Inn. The only time I had seen my daughter was when my parents brought her to visit. Most blatant of all, during the whole time I'd been awake, George hadn't once stepped into my room.

Night after night, I thought about his absence. I wondered what I would have done if the tables had been turned. Would I have been able to witness the damage done to the body of the person I loved? Would I have stood by administering comfort if my husband had been unable to reciprocate? Would I have been willing to make visits, knowing that I'd never hear a word from the mouth of the man I'd intended to spend the rest of my life with?

I didn't know how to answer these questions. If it had been Jim who had suffered the strokes, I don't think I would have been able to offer committed support. There wasn't a strong bond between us. George and I had a different kind of relationship. We weren't kids when we married. The seven years that intervened between my first and second marriages made me realize that I'd acted childishly by running off with André. After I'd returned from the trip with André, I thought that I'd be branded a harlot and wouldn't be able to find a second husband. I worried that I'd always be alone, especially since I was a divorcée, and that I'd never realize my dream of being a mother.

During these years, though I'd been asked out many times, I'd always refused. I had thought George was different from the other men I'd met. He seemed stable and grounded, easy to understand. He was an excellent provider. He not only bought the house on Roosevelt Street but furnished it. He was able to support not only me and Judy but also our two foster children. Yet I raged at his abandonment of me.

Though people had wondered, when I married George, why I'd wed a man who wasn't even good looking, I thought their views a preposterous and shallow way of regarding love. Jim had been easily the most handsome man I'd met. Yet he didn't truly care for me, as I, ultimately, didn't care for him. George was not shallow. I treated him with respect, and he reciprocated. If it hadn't been for the strokes, I have no doubt that we would still be in love.

. . .

One month before the bombing of Pearl Harbor, when I was almost seven, Dad turned our cellar into a bomb shelter. He built a bin out of sheet metal and stocked the bin with coal. "To keep us safe and warm if the damn Nazis land," he said, in his slight Hungarian accent. "If they take one step onto my land, I'll kill the bastards cold." He laid cinder blocks out in a raised row and told Mom to pile blankets on top of the makeshift bed. Then Dad stocked his guns and a box of ammunition in a wooden cabinet he took from his shop and screwed into one wall of the cellar.

Mom did her own stocking: knives with which to protect ourselves (from what, I didn't know), canned goods all in a neat row with the labels turned out, sealed jugs of water, and a box of clothes we'd be able to change into when the time came. She put toiletry goods next to the portable toilet Dad brought in, and an emergency first-aid kit.

We'd have drills in which Dad would blow a whistle and we'd have to run into the dark cellar, which smelled of mold and gasoline and decayed fruit. It was scary to me because it made me think of being buried deep in the earth. The cellar was damp, and my eyes had to adjust to the light coming through a crack in the door atop the eight steps. I worried that we'd get stuck down there, that the door wouldn't open and we'd all suffocate.

After we'd climbed down the stairs and our eyes had had a chance to adjust, we'd find our assigned places. Dad would bolt the door. The dark was so dense that I couldn't see my own hand in front of my face, and the deep silence made my bones ache. This darkness paralyzed me, as at school when the other children gathered in a circle around Joan and me and called us "Nazi Pollacks" and "dumb foreigners" and threatened to beat us up.

Shame had my father's face and my mother's Polish accent. It smelled of damp concrete and rotten apples, and it crawled like worms over a dead body. It smelled of powder shot from the end of Father's .22 rifle and of the split cords of wood out back, behind Father's junkyard where we used to hide when Dad got out his black belt. At school I felt like an alien from another planet, and at home I worried about saying or doing the wrong things. My schoolmates' cruelty, my mother's bad English, Dad's guns, Joanie's blood on the Skpansky's oak tree, and the new drama of the bomb shelter and impending war merged in my mind to create a feeling of shame.

My shame turned into silences at school and attention-generating antics at home. I'd take a swig of Dad's whiskey and purposely leave the cap off of the bottle. And since I blamed myself for my father's drinking and his bad temper, I'd seclude myself in my room and feel my shame in isolation.

Then Pearl Harbor was bombed. Upon hearing the news, Dad flew into a rage, railing against the Japanese and the Germans. I learned plenty of cuss words that night, as Dad got out his guns, which he polished and loaded, and then checked the bolt on the cellar door. He told us to go down into the shelter to keep safe. Vowing to kill the enemies himself, if necessary, he made it clear that Franklin Roosevelt and Winston Churchill were the heroes he'd stand behind.

Down in the cellar, I huddled with Mom and Joan and Midge, thinking the world was going to end with us there in the dark, the smell of shame and banishment as sweet as the apples rotting around us.

. . .

I lay flat, and the world became as dark as the underground cellar. The world wasn't going to end. But my life in it had. I watched the two nurses complete their duties, lowering my bed down by its crank. I was drowsy from the drugs injected into me and couldn't keep my eyes open. I fell asleep for my first night in room D-11.

Chapter Seven

SUCK IT IN
AND SPIT IT OUT

Birds fly above me, I hear them circling.
Sun's beams wait at my sill
And I taste my breakfast going
Down. Suck it in, now
Circle it around your
Mouth. Spit it out.
Brazen things.
Hateful things.

I heard someone slandering me.
Suck it in and churn it.
Spit it out. Now that's what
It's all about.
Birds closing in on me.
I sucked it in and spit it out
And turned around
Cuz that's what it's all about.

For the next ten years the D ward remained my un-wanted home. Though I lived for short stints on the B and C wards, I always got transferred back to the D ward, due to recurring bouts of pneumonia.

That first week back from Bellevue, as my lungs cleared and my fever subsided, I figured that the D ward was for sickness and minor setbacks for people with major paralysis.

The woman wheezed in the bed to my right. A nurse wheeled a respirator to her and secured a clear mask over her nose and mouth so the machine breathed for her. Air was our element now. We were snowed in, walled in cold stone too high to climb, even if we had hands for gripping and legs for skirting sheer ice.

At night, the room emptied of color, shape, and all sound but that of breathing. It was a persistent sound, the whistle of wind through a crevice in stone. I imagined that if any of us had been able to walk to that fissure and peer through at what lay beyond it, we might have seen a world of field and ocean, a world of color and form. And there, with our palms pressed against the stone and our eyes fo-cused on the miracle of the world beyond us, we might have resumed our normal breathing.

In that room of complete darkness, I felt afraid to sleep, to submit to dreams and memories and regrets just beyond my field of vision. So I lay in bed and thought, questioned, imagined what might have happened to cause the breakdown of my body. What had caused my limbs to bend and my bones to twist? In my mind, I interrogated my family and my husband. Why am I unable to speak? Where is everyone?

Thought was my bane. I remembered my mother saying the word *hemorrhage*, and the nurse telling my sister about *strokes*. I knew my paralysis had something to do with these words. If I'd been reduced to twisted limbs and a mind that couldn't think or register pain, or if I'd been a "vegetable," as a nurse once put it, I'd never regret the loss of my hands and feet. If I couldn't think, I'd never even know the difference between life and death.

But I could think, all night, if I cared to. Inside my sealed tent, the air was purified of all elements of danger. The room was emptied of everything I'd once considered living—words, voices, bodies touching and hands caressing and normal food and the feel of air in my hair as I raced my convertible down Sunrise Highway and felt the accelerator against my foot, the efficient hum of the engine and silky roll of the tires on the pavement in my ears and the light grip of the wheel in my hands as I rounded the final stretch. I heard the crowd and leaned forward, as if the deciding factor would be the use of my own body, and I felt the wheel against my chest, the driver's uniform Father had once worn snug against my breasts and all the breath in me used for the pushing forward, the winning, holding it in as I crossed the imaginary finish line, the first woman to win the Grand Prix. The lifeless room was all I had now.

In the day's first light, a nurse cranked my bed up. I

looked at her slender fingers and saw the fuchsia polish she must have painted on her nails the previous night. I felt so much anger that I blamed her. I blamed my husband for not getting me to a doctor on time. I blamed my mother and father for not giving me a proper upbringing, the kids at school for ridiculing me, doctors and nurses and ambulance drivers and God. I blamed them all until my head ached from so much unfounded accusation. I thought I was going to go insane with the anger I felt, but then I realized how wrong it was to blame others for my misfortune. No one had caused my body's breakdown. But what was I to do with the anger I could not express?

Again, no answer presented itself, and I wished to die rather than to be forced to endure alone the suffering, the humiliation, the gnawing in my legs and the burning in my feet. I couldn't understand why Joanie and the other members of my family weren't here, especially after I'd just survived the pneumonia. If they really thought I was cognitive, why wouldn't they be here supporting me? Though I realized that raising a family, as Joan was doing, was difficult and time-consuming, I didn't understand how my sister, whom I'd always considered my best friend, could leave me to waste away, alone.

Anything would have been better than being alive and aware of the nurse who hated her assumed responsibility for my life. She carted me off to the shower without ever touching me compassionately or looking me in the eye. She didn't even notice that I was drowning in my own lungs. Anything would be better than the water thumping against my neck and chest while her hands turned me on my side, and I felt the cloth covering fall off the tube in my throat.

A drop of water slipped into the tube. *This is it*, I thought, *this is my chance*. I turned my neck enough to let more water drizzle into the tube. I leaned my head back as far as I could, feeling the water go down my throat. *Yes, it's going to happen. Yes, I'm going to drown now. Yes, I'll be free of this pain*. I thought about how little water it would take to drown me and how quickly my dying would be over. I choked. I gagged. All the water came out of my lungs, and the nurse once again covered the tube with the cloth.

Back in my room, I was dressed and put into bed. I had failed to die. Now I would lie here until someone came to change my diaper or feed me. Perhaps nothing would happen, and I'd just remain still.

No sooner had I thought that I might lie here until I was taken for dead when a nurse's aide walked into my room. She started slamming things around—the garbage pail, my feeder—and as she slid the tray from the suction machine in the wall beside my bed, she groaned. She took the tray to the sink and emptied the contents down the drain. As she arranged things back into order, another aide came to help her.

"Damn nuisance, that's what I call it," the second aide announced upon entering the room.

"No lie," said the first. "I don't even know why they bother anymore. She's been this way more than four years now. And there ain't no miracles on God's green earth, I'm tellin' you. Bringing the daughter this time, no less."

I lit up bright as the sun at the word *daughter*.

The aide scrubbed some of my liquid diet, hardened to a crust, from the table beside my bed, where three times a day someone regulated my feeding.

"Imagine being blessed with a pile of bones for a mother," chimed in the second aide. I stopped listening and remembered the one time I'd seen Judy since I woke up. She'd been afraid of me, of the condition I was in. I'm sure the tube in my throat scared her, and the one protruding from my nose made me monstrous to my little girl.

I lay imagining how Judy would react now that she was a little older. I wondered who would bring her and whether George's sister, Mae, was taking good care of her. I figured that she must have started school by now. I wondered what food she liked best and whether she'd seen Mickey Mouse. Had she learned how to swim yet? I was trying to calculate how old she was when the doors to my room swung open. To my astonishment, George walked in.

He was wearing a golf cap and a maroon jacket with Peninsula Golf Club written over the left pocket. He looked older than I remembered. He'd lost most of his hair, and his skin wrinkled into crow's feet around his eyes. Yet his eyes still had the sparkle that had first attracted me, still conveyed patience and a firmness in making decisions. One thing I'd learned to depend on was that when George made a decision, nothing could change his mind.

Yet now, when I looked at him, the virtues I had once seen became worthless. How could a man leave his wife alone in a hospital, regardless of her condition? Whatever had caused him to do this, he too was in pain. Before the strokes, I think there was nothing he wouldn't have done for me. That's how in love we were. Oftentimes, back when we were first married and before Judy had been born, whether we were driving on a Sunday afternoon in George's black coupe, strolling through the quiet streets of Inwood, or hitting balls at the golf range, we were happy just being together.

Now, with silence imposed on us, it surprised me how little affection I felt, even though I had once loved him. As he stood a few feet away from my bed and held Judy by the hand, I thought, *Why has he picked now to come? Why didn't he just stay away forever so I could forget him?*

George led Judy closer to me, and I started to cry. The first thing I noticed about my daughter was how big she'd gotten. Her hair had darkened to chestnut brown. It was longer than I had remembered—almost down to her shoulders—and she had it tied back with a pink ribbon. She was wearing a pink dress I didn't recognize, with white shoes and socks. She looked healthy and well cared for. She must be five or six years old, I thought.

George must have felt nervous. At first, he stared at the floor and didn't speak. He glanced down at me, then looked out the window. He started making practice swings with an imaginary golf club, an old habit of his that used to drive me crazy. Even though he thought I couldn't understand him, he spoke to me.

"Yep, I work in Massapequa. At the new golf club. I'm head golf pro now."

I wondered what had happened to his job at the Lawrence Country Club. For what seemed like twenty minutes, he went on about his game, how he was shooting and who his new clients were. I thought how one of those rich ladies from Lawrence had probably taken my place. No wonder that no one but my mother had mentioned him since I woke up, and all she could do was curse him.

He paused once more and looked out the window. He glanced down at Judy, who was staring at me. I was torn in two: part of me was full of love and adoration for my little girl, while the other half was cursing George, wondering how he could have been so in love with me and then dropped me when I needed him most. Yet I tried not to show my anger, out of fear that I'd scare Judy.

The half an hour that George stood by my bed was an emotional hell. I wanted to be happy to see him, thankful that he'd brought my daughter to visit. But I was so angry and confused about why he'd been absent that all I could do was loathe him. My anger was at the surface of my skin. If I could have lashed out, either verbally or physically, I wouldn't have hesitated for a second. I'd been awake for four years. I had thought, at first, that he'd fallen in love with someone else. Then I'd reconsidered. It would be difficult to raise Judy and take care of his sisters if there was another woman around. I figured it must be deeper than that and not such an easy explanation. Maybe I was now so unrecognizable that he couldn't bear to see me.

He didn't touch my hand or try to comfort me. He continued practicing his golf swing. I listened to George, who seemed oblivious to my paralysis, go on and on. Out of consideration for Judy, I tried to remain as still as possible, holding back my tears. For the first time since I'd been trapped inside my body, I tried not to move when others were near me. I wanted Judy to be as comfortable as possible. I thought that if I moved or cried, she'd withdraw and I'd never see her again.

George raised his arm to make another swing, and I saw that he wasn't wearing his wedding ring. Even though it was possible that mine had been taken off to prevent it from being stolen, George had obviously taken his ring off himself. I knew then what I'd refused to accept since I'd noticed my wedding band missing that day in the shower: George no longer loved me. Our marriage was over.

I spiraled into the worst depression of my life. I kept imagining another woman sleeping in my bed. George made another swing toward the hallway beyond the glass partition, and I wanted to kill him. The longer he stood there, the more jealous and angry I became. Remembering my own abandonment of my first husband, I suddenly felt a terrible sense of remorse. Only at that moment, in the midst of my own rage and suffering, did I realize how much pain I'd caused Jim.

George stopped swinging. He looked down at me, then over at Judy. He talked some more about golf, then glanced out into the hall. A nurse came in to check on the woman in the bed across from me, but George didn't speak to her. Judy started getting impatient and tugged at George's sleeve.

"Well, we'd better go now," he said. "Judy has homework to do."

He looked at her, and I realized that I was missing my daughter's life. I wanted to be the one helping her with her homework. I wanted to show her how to braid her hair and what kind of clothes to wear. She was the most beautiful child I'd ever seen. For a moment I forgave George. I marveled that the two of us had produced such a lovely girl.

"Judy, kiss your mother good-bye," he said.

He held her up so she could kiss me. Her white shoes were spotless. George brought her close. I saw how her green eyes sparkled in the light. She still had her baby teeth. I felt her lips brush lightly against my cheek. Though I wanted that kiss to last forever, it was as quick as the blink of an eye.

George put Judy down. He looked at me, then glanced toward the door. He took Judy by the hand, looked down at the floor, and said good-bye. The two of them walked into the hall, neither looking back. Then and there, I made plans for war.

. . .

The day after George and Judy's visit, two nurses came into the room. "She's had a bad bout of respiratory insufficiency, but now her lungs are clear," I heard one of them say. "They want her transferred out of ICU and onto the C ward." They hooked me to the lifter, raised me up, and transported me on another gurney to the C ward, room 41.

The afternoon I was moved, a nurse I'd never seen before came into my room. She held a small stick in her hand. She said in a voice that was sweet but with a caustic edge, "I'm not going to hurt you. I just want to clean your teeth."

Clean my teeth! That was about the last thing on my mind. I'd been in this hospital more than four years, and for the first time someone was worried about sugar rotting my teeth! What struck me as funny was not only her announcement but also the fact that this woman was talking to me. Besides the nurse who spoke to me the first time I had pneumonia, this was the only time anyone on the hospital staff had ever said anything to me, let alone thought about my teeth. The others took it for granted that I was a sack of mud who never needed her teeth cleaned.

"Don't worry, I'm not going to hurt you."

I thought, *The hell you're not. I've been lying here how many years, and now they want to start my personalized hygiene program? How dare they consider it!*

The nurse came over to my bed. She wore glasses and had on an immaculate white uniform, over which she wore a clear plastic apron. My mind went wild with the possibilities.

She held that stick as if it were a knife. I didn't trust what she was going to do to me. Every time someone did something—anything—I felt pain. Smiling, she put a rubber glove on each hand. Stupid idiot, I thought. Must be her first day—that's why she's talking to me.

She came close to me, and I screamed. "Don't worry," she said, "I'm not going to hurt you. Just tell me if you feel any pain."

As I continued to scream, she put the stick and two of her fingers into my mouth. I'm going to teach them all a lesson, I thought. And then I heard another voice inside me say, "That's not nice." *Screw nice*, I thought.

"I'm going to circle my fingers in your mouth and check your teeth. If you need to spit, just let me know."

I felt her fingers in my mouth. She held my tongue down with the stick, touched my gums, and started tapping my teeth. I guess she was checking to see which ones needed cleaning, but I didn't have patience for her pleasantries. After all, my husband had come in the day before and had proved that he cared only about his golf game. My daughter didn't seem to know me.

I waited until the nurse had her fingers deep in my mouth. I felt the tip of her finger along my tongue. She was bending over me, her face close to mine. That's when I bit down as hard as I could. *With this bite*, I thought, *I'm going to get even with everyone*. All the anger and resentment that I felt about my family abandoning me and the people around me treating me less than human went into that bite. I bit down in fear of never being understood. I bit down in an effort to communicate that I didn't want her poking her fingers in my mouth.

The nurse's eyes got very wide, her mouth flew open, and she jumped away from me while letting out a blood-curdling scream and exclaiming, "You bit me!"

No kidding, I thought.

She peeled off her rubber glove and hurried out. I heard her yell, "The one in C-41 bit me!" I smiled, satisfied that I had accomplished something that day.

. . .

This began my new career—finding ways to make people realize that I was cognitive. Like anyone else, I didn't want people to do things to me without asking my permission. After all, my body was still my own.

I became adept not only at biting and screaming but also at using many direct forms of nonverbal communication. I learned to howl with a little volume as I leaned forward and clenched my arms as tightly as possible to my chest to get people to stop doing something. I learned to become limp so I wasn't as easy to turn over and manipulate. When people spoke negatively about me, I'd cry so much that I'd distract them. Best of all was my new trick: vomiting.

A few years before I was paralyzed, I read an article in the newspaper that made me become a vegetarian. It was the story of a crazy man who abused his girlfriend. One day she did something that made him go berserk. When she came home that night, he was waiting for her. He killed her, methodically cut her up, and ate the pieces. The moment I read this, I ran to the bathroom and threw up. Thereafter, every time I thought of this heinous act, I'd get queasy. If I didn't stop thinking of it, I'd be sick.

Now, I figured that I could use this sensitivity to my advantage. The next time someone touched me in a way I found offensive, I thought of that man brutalizing his girlfriend. Sure enough, I threw up—all over a nurse's arm. That was victory number two.

. . .

Though my actions expressed my feelings in no uncertain terms, there were consequences. The nurses and aides became even more hostile to me. Most of the things they did were small, like leaving me wet longer than usual or pinching me "accidentally" when they changed my diaper. I think they did it because they all thought that I was not functioning mentally and that they didn't have anything to lose. Since I couldn't speak for myself or write anything down or use sign language, they didn't need to worry about being caught.

My anger was not constant, though. When it ebbed, I retreated into a dark place inside me where no light was ever seen, no kiss given. I started thinking of myself as undeserving of affection. This feeling spiraled down until I considered myself unworthy of life itself. Darkness pervaded every inch of space around me until I couldn't see clearly. I entered a long, dark tunnel.

One evening, an aide came to change me. Besides the two women sleeping, no one else was in the room. As soon as the aide drew aside the curtain, she turned and looked me right in the face.

"You pull any of that shit with me, and I'll show you what's comin'. And don't think that just cuz you're some poor paralyzed thing that I won't. Cuz I will." She said it the way some people scold their dogs.

She's mad that she's on the twilight shift, I thought. She doesn't want to take care of me.

She pulled my shoulder toward her, hard. I felt a pain bite down my left side. I started to cry.

"If you don't stop crying right now and let me do this stupid job, I'm going to smack you so hard you won't know what hit you."

When I didn't quit crying, she muttered, "Pain in the ass." Then she raised her hand and slapped my face.

I cried all the more.

She hit me again. "That'll give you something to cry about, you baby."

I felt myself shutting off from the world, closing down emotionally. Everything went black. I felt like I was suffocating in the dark earth while the aide piled more dirt on top of me.

She snatched the diaper out from under me and pulled my legs open. She wiped me hard, then pinned another diaper on me. It was too tight, and it irritated my skin. She ignored my cries, opened the curtain, and left the room without saying another word.

. . .

In the dream that night, I was getting Judy ready to take her to the doctor's office. I dressed her in a new outfit, a white dress with white high-top shoes. I kept thinking that Judy's feet were smaller than the feet of the doll my sister Midge used to play with when we were little girls. As I dressed her, our black Labrador puppy bounded into the room and tried to jump on my bed.

The dream shifted, and I closed the door of our house on Roosevelt Street. With Judy in my arms, I walked to my blue Oldsmobile convertible. I put Judy in the seat beside me, and we drove away.

We were almost to the doctor's when I noticed another car trailing us. I started driving very fast, but I couldn't lose that car. Judy began to cry. She wailed, and I could hear nothing but her screams. I pulled to the side of the road.

As the car stopped, a man I'd never seen before appeared at my window. He told me to get out of the car. I reached over to take Judy out, but the man told me to leave her and said, "You won't need her where you're going."

I climbed out of the car, and he grabbed me gruffly by

the arm. He pushed me against the door. Judy's face was pressed against the glass, as if she were under water. The man started leading me to his car.

"My baby," I screamed, "who's going to take care of my baby!" I tried to hit him. He took a rope from his pocket and tied my hands together.

"Get in, lady. And don't make a scene." He pushed me into the car.

Through the windshield, I saw Judy's head. "Please let me have my baby," I pleaded, just before I slipped from the man's grip and flew up into the sky.

I awoke from the dream. I realized that the crying wasn't from Judy but from the person who had just been moved into the bed next to mine.

Julia, age 17, 1952. *Courtesy of the author.*

Julia's parents, Joseph and Mary Horwat, in front of their John Street home in Inwood, Long Island, in 1942.
Courtesy of the author.

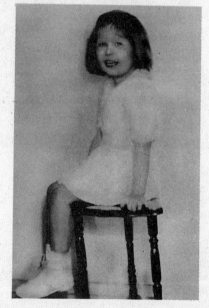

Julia, age 4, 1939.
Photo by Stella Horwat.

Julia with her father's
1930 Packard.
Photo by Joan Bennettson.

At Roaches Beach, 1955.
Photo by Joseph Horwat.

After Arlene Kraat discovers that Julia is cognitive, she teaches her how to communicate with a letter board she designed for Julia, circa 1976. *Photo by Joyce Sabari.*

Julia uses Joyce Sabari's headstick pointer to read a book in Goldwater Hospital's library, 1976. *Courtesy of Arlene Kraat.*

Arlene in 1995. She has achieved international renown for her work in augmentative communications.
Photo by Gary Friedman. © 1995 Los Angeles Times. *Reprinted by permission.*

Joyce Sabari in 1996.
Courtesy of Joyce Sabari.

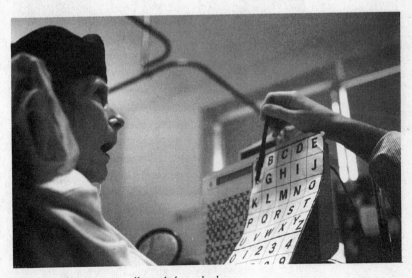

Julia raises her eyes to spell words letter by letter.
Photo by Gary Friedman. 1995 Los Angeles Times. *Reprinted by permission.*

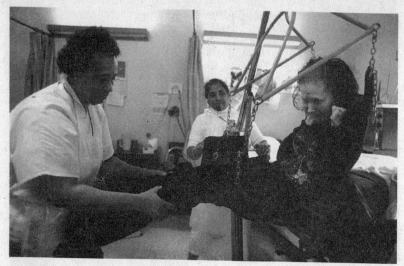

Two nurse's aides on the A ward use the Hoyer lift to position Julia in her wheelchair. *Photo by Gary Friedman.* © 1995 Los Angeles Times. *Reprinted by permission.*

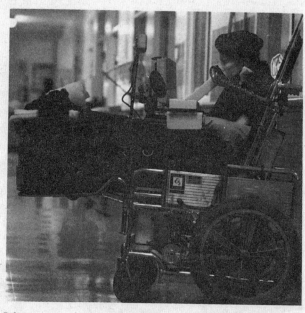

Julia maneuvers her wheelchair through the corridors of Goldwater Hospital. *Photo by Gary Friedman.* © 1995 Los Angeles Times. *Reprinted by permission.*

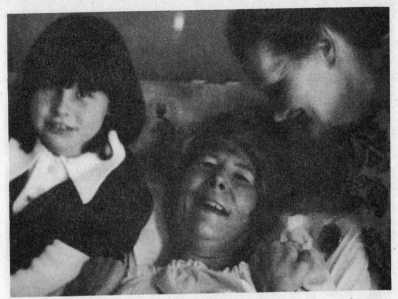

Judy, age 10, and Julia's mother dress Julia up during a visit to the C ward in 1975. *Photo by Linda Tropiano.*

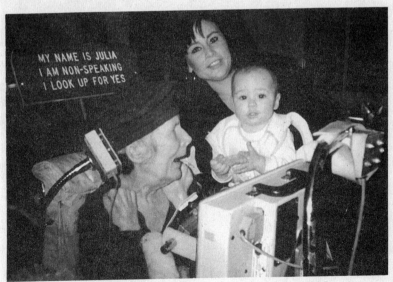

MY NAME IS JULIA
I AM NON-SPEAKING
I LOOK UP FOR YES

Judy surprises Julia with her grandson, Harrison, in December 1995.
Courtesy of the author.

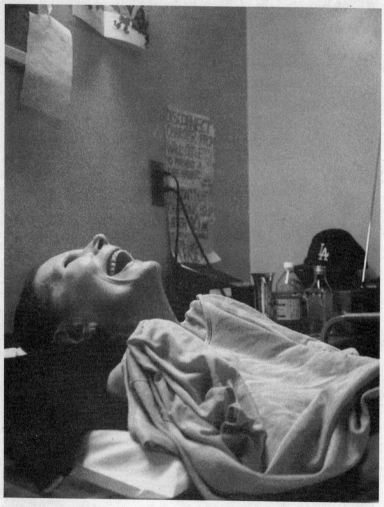

Laughter in the A ward. *Photo by Gary Friedman.* © 1995 Los Angeles Times. *Reprinted by permission.*

Chapter Eight

DREAMING YOU

Along the lonely road I walked
A flock! of birds did I see
Their wings fluttered and I heard
Your name, as they flew away from me.
I saw a rocket with your name!
Reached up and grabbed it
Shoved it in my pocket
Walked back to my lonely room.
The rain fell on my window pane
Rain sang your name
Tell me if I'm going insane
Or am just madly in love
With your name.

Night and day, winter and summer, the days melted shapelessly together. My sister and mother visited less often. Each time they came, they were quieter. When my bed was raised, I saw their faces furrowed in sorrow, as

if they didn't have any choice but to believe the hospital
staff's prognosis: my case was hopeless. Joan tried for a
while longer to convince the nurses that I was alive. But she
told my mother that she was losing ground and couldn't
persuade them that I was mentally aware. She even began to
believe herself that her jokes and my corresponding change
of expression had been a hopeful wish.

Seasons revolved, no clock ticked, and I was moved
like a mattress people kept sitting on from A-4I to ICU,
D-2I to C-32, B-3I to D-II.

One snowy afternoon about six years after I woke up
from the coma, a nurse with a crooked nose and a missing
front tooth carried a package into my room.

"Pampers," she mumbled to herself, "a new kind of
diaper."

When she said the word *pampers*, I laughed hysterically
to myself. Silently, inwardly, my laugh caused my ribs to jar.
I felt a vibration down to my kneecaps, shins, toe joints. I
was laughing my full-fledged quadriplegic laugh at being
pampered in a place where no one even looked at me when
they strapped a diaper too tight to my crotch, where they
called me a crybaby and shot shower water down the tube
in my throat.

For six years, a hand pulled the crank and my bed rose
to greet the laughable day. Someone rolled me onto my
stomach, and my face struck the bed rail. I wailed while two
nurses and a man I'd never seen before hoisted me onto a
black-padded gurney covered with a cold sheet. I was wear-

ing a light cotton gown no one had bothered to tie at the neck. I was rolling my head from side to side and moving my eyes. I wanted to know where they were taking me.

They rolled me into a room I'd never seen before and lifted me onto a table. Two women got on either side of me, each with her hands beneath my arms. Neither of them said anything to me. Someone counted to three, and the women tried to make my body sit up. As I screamed in pain, neither therapist stopped bending my back. They heaved against me, pulling my arms away from my chest. My shoulders contracted, and the muscles went tight. They bent and turned me, then stretched out my legs and bent them back. After searching a minute to find my left knee-cap, they touched it and tried to relocate it. When they couldn't, they moved up to my hands and attempted to un-curl my fingers. I screamed and felt excruciating pain. I hoped to pass out.

But the pain kept me conscious. They tried to move my legs up and down, turning my sockets. They continued down to my ankles, splaying my toes. I felt a burning sen-sation along the length of each leg. Though my feet veered inward, toward the center of my body, they wanted to force alignment. When they bent my feet, I wanted to die.

I screamed for them to stop. They continued. They spoke to each other in technical jargon. "Passive ROM in forearm pronation," "forearm supination," "shoulder ab-duction to thirty degrees"—none of this made sense to me.

Though my hands were tighter than loaded springs,

the therapists again attempted to open them. Neither one recognized that I was screaming because the pain was so severe. They bent each of my fingers, one by one, until they got my left hand to move.

"You see," one said to the other, "progress!"

The one who said this took a clipboard and wrote something down.

"That's it for today. Let's get this mad dog back to her cage."

Three weeks passed before I was given any other "therapy." One morning, a nurse rolled me over in bed to give me a sponge bath. After she finished washing me, she dressed me in a clean gown and what appeared to be men's pajama pants.

She put the lifting pad behind me and hoisted me into the air. A second nurse brought in a wheelchair.

I started to scream in my half-muted way, remembering what it had been like when they had tried to sit me up three weeks earlier. This chair is much steeper than my back can bend, I thought. There's no way they're going to get me in that.

The one rolling the chair positioned it beneath me. When they raised me out of the Hoyer lift, I screamed to get them to stop. I was trying to break through, to communicate somehow that what they were doing was unacceptable because of the extreme pain involved. I just wanted them to stop.

They lowered me down too fast, and I almost fell to

the ground. I was hysterical with fear. They slowed my descent, and I felt myself go down the last few inches. I noticed a thin layer of padding on the chair's seat, but it was not enough to lessen the pain searing down my back. *If there's a God*, I thought, *or any sense to this life, please make them stop.*

They did not stop. The back of the chair was sloped at that impossible angle, and the foot rests were parallel with the ground. My body's natural inclination was to remain supine because my spine simply could no longer curve. But the nurses acted as if they didn't understand this. Though I cried and attempted to move any part of my body to relieve the pain flaring up my back, they remained inert beside me. I screamed like I'd never screamed before. This was the worst pain I'd known in my life. I prayed to black out.

Suddenly, as I was wailing to get out of the chair, I discovered that I could move my hips a tiny increment and straighten my back just enough to cause my body to slide down, decreasing the amount of skin surface making contact with the chair. This, I figured, would relieve some of the pain blazing along my back and buttocks. I concentrated hard, straining to move my whole body about half an inch. The nurses stood there, watching me cry and wiggle and slide down in the chair, never realizing that I was trying to move, not to spite them but to save myself from further torture. As I slid down, I felt proud—I'd succeeded in moving my own body!

When I had slipped almost completely out of the

chair, one of the nurses left the room. She came back with an armful of sheets. Then the two of them worked together, rolling the sheets into thick strips like ropes. They did this with four separate sheets and then started tying my legs to the chair. They wrapped one sheet around my right ankle, making a tight knot. They tied my left leg in the same way. They moved up to my waist and tied me to the back of the chair.

As I writhed in pain, the two of them stood looking at me. "That oughta hold 'er," one of them said, just before she wheeled me into the main hall.

Even tied down in the chair, I was able to wiggle my hips and arch my back enough to slide down inch by inch. When the nurses saw me doing this, one of them rushed over, called me a "wicked witch" in front of the other people in the hall, and wheeled me back to my room. Despite the pain, I smiled to myself: I had discovered a way to move my own body.

. . .

That night, I felt so depressed that I wanted to kill myself. If I could have reached for a knife, or crawled to the window and opened it myself, or held a syringe and filled it with strychnine, I would not have hesitated.

That's when I got another idea of how to kill myself.

I had three pillows, a small one on top of two larger ones. When they put me down for the night, they arranged the pillows so the small one was on top of the other two. There were a few hours between the time the nurses thought I'd go to sleep and midnight, when they made their rounds and shone a flashlight on each person's face. I decided that after they turned out the light, I'd go to work: I'd wiggle the small pillow over my face, hold my breath, and try to smother myself.

I tried, but no matter what I did, I couldn't cover my whole face—nose, mouth, tube in my throat—all at once. The tube kept foiling me by allowing air to pass into my throat, even when I held my breath. I'd almost get my face covered by the pillow, but the tube stuck out too far. I couldn't cover its opening. The pillows became drenched with sweat, and I felt more frustrated with each attempt to smother myself. No matter how long I held my breath, that hole kept me alive.

While I lay thoroughly frustrated in the dark, Grandma Horwat appeared a second time. Unlike before, I could see only her face and her penetrating eyes. Those eyes looked at me the way they did the night she stood on the embankment, holding out her hand.

"Come, Julie," she said in the same musical voice, "come to Nana."

I watched her lips form those words. I wanted to take her hand and follow her to a land of no pain—"Heaven," she used to call it. But in this vision I had no physical form. I could hear her, and I was certain that she knew I was there, yet my body had no substance. I was made of air.

As in the previous vision, Nana knew what I was thinking. As soon as I thought, *I wish I had been in the coal shaft when the accident happened*, I knew Nana understood that these words referred to the time before I was born when there had been an accident at the Pittsburgh coal mines, where my father used to work. Though my father wasn't injured, that calamity killed almost a hundred miners. Even though I hadn't thought of this accident since my father had told me about it many years before, Nana knew that I wanted to suffocate, as those men had, deep in the earth. To me it was the perfect way to die, painlessly, instantly, without effort. Just as I thought this, Nana faded away, leaving me alone in my dark tunnel.

. . .

Morning is a black dress approaching and Grandma Horwat gone. A woman is a green triangle who speaks through a sleeve.

"Hello, Mrs. Televaro," says a voice I don't recognize. "Can you hear me?"

I want to close my eyes and continue dreaming. Despite the mispronunciation of my name, the tenderness in this voice makes me listen.

A warm hand touches my cheek. "Can you hear me, Mrs. Tavalaro?" she repeats, this time getting my name right.

Slowly, mistrustfully, I look up. I see a woman with a

slender face, high cheekbones, kind brown eyes, and light brown hair down past her shoulders. I realize I've seen her five or six times before, passing in the hall outside the glass partition.

"I'm Arlene Kraat from speech therapy. We're going to see if you can talk."

She pauses, and I feel like I'm experiencing a dream about to end with me the fool and the hero turning her back and walking out the door.

"Can you close your eyes, Mrs. Tavalaro?"

With these words, I'm shocked back into reality. This is no dream: I'm actually being spoken *to*. I close my eyes. I open them and see Arlene's face.

"Can you blink twice?"

I do it.

Silence fills the space between us. Her face shows shock and grief and happiness at once. In the previous six years, no one had thought to ask me these simple questions.

"Okay, Mrs. Tavalaro. I'd like you to respond with eye movements. Can you move your eyes up, like this?" She rolls her eyes toward her forehead.

I watch her do this. Then, with a quick movement of my eyes, I feel my mind rise from the ocean depths of pain. For the first time in six years, I feel whole.

"Excellent," Arlene says. "Now, I'd like to ask you a question, Mrs. Tavalaro. To respond, move your eyes up for *yes* and down for *no*.

To show that I understand, I raise my eyes.

"Exactly. Good. What is the first letter of your name?"

She starts reciting the alphabet. When she gets to "J," I raise my eyes.

Arlene makes a smile so big that I feel hope for the first time since Joanie screamed at the nurse almost six years before. Though it might come to nothing, I decide to trust her.

Each of her hands goes into a pocket of her white jacket. She pulls them out and holds her hands in the air before me. Each hand grips a small object.

"Julia, which of these would be better to write with?" She looks intently at me now, as if she can't believe this is happening any more than I. She repeats her question.

I know the answer, but I'm stuck on the word *Julia.* Its sound tumbles in my mind like a red plum falling into a metal bucket.

I look at her face again. Her left hand holds the crayon up. "This one?"

I look down for *no.*

"This one?" she asks, holding the pencil in the air.

I look up for *yes.*

She smiles at my response, then places the crayon back in her left pocket. She brushes her hair behind her ear with her thumb and forefinger. I hear the even rhythm of her breathing. She holds the pencil aloft once more.

I look up once more.

She takes a clipboard and writes something with the pencil. When she stops writing, she reaches into her pocket and takes out a tiny flashlight. "I'd like to use this to check your mouth and throat. Maybe I can help you communicate. Is that all right with you, Julia?"

I raise my eyes for *yes*, hardly able to believe that someone is asking permission before she does something to me.

Resting her palm against my forehead, Arlene takes the flashlight, leans down over me, and gently touches the sides of my throat. Her hands feel warm and unhurried. Everything about her—her posture as she bends over and shines the light into my throat, her understanding tone of voice, her smile—indicates that she cares about improving my life. Never once does she treat me as less than her equal. I feel a mutual concern for her and a feeling of kinship, as if she's my sister.

"Try to say 'hello,' Julia."

I strain so hard that it hurts. Yet I'm unsuccessful in making anything more than a muffled groan.

"Okay," Arlene says, writing something on the clipboard. The sound of her pencil moving across the paper soothes me.

This is real! I think. *She's going to do something to help me.*

She puts the flashlight back in her pocket, then looks me directly in the eyes. "How would you like to have meals again and receive phone calls from your parents? How would you like to talk?"

I stare at her as if she's crazy. Yet I feel hopeful. Maybe Arlene can do something that will enable me to speak. Because she treats me with kindness, I feel human for the first time in years.

After a moment of thinking about what she's just asked, I get excited. I think how I'd love to devour a plate of lasagna and a tall vodka collins. I think how I'd love to yell at the top of my lungs when the next person calls me "Queen Bee" or spurts water down the hole in my throat. I revel at the idea of inviting my husband to visit so I can ask him why he left me alone here. I think how I'd love to alert the proper authorities about the mistreatment I've received by those who hold my life in their hands. I smile at the endless prospects.

Arlene smiles back. "It's been quite a lot for one day, don't you think, Julia?"

I look down for *no*.

She laughs.

"You sure are enthusiastic. I admire your spunk. How would you like it if I spoke to the heads of speech and OT [occupational therapy], in the hopes of placing you on an active treatment program?"

Without hesitation, I raise my eyes.

"First, we'll have to do some broader evaluations," Arlene continues, taking out an appointment book. As she writes, I watch her fingers grasp the pencil. "I'm going to see if we can arrange for you to attend some hospital activities."

I look up to express my approval.

"Good to meet you, Julia. See you in OT."

Chapter Nine

WISH

I wish I could walk talk again.
I wish I could take your hand in mine
as your hand is mine. I wish
I could hold your body next to mine
for just a while, so we could be two
making one, and we could wish.

A week later, as soon as I saw a nurse rolling the wheelchair into my room, I forgot all about going to OT.
I started to panic. The memory of the time I'd been tied
into a chair came flooding back, and I felt afraid of the pain.
Two nurses trundled the Hoyer lift over to me, hooked the
pad behind me, and hoisted me into the air. Without
knowing anything except what I'd overheard, I was set in
the seat and tied down with six sheets.

The pain was excruciating. I started to scream but
hardly any sound came out. Someone said, "You see, she's
at it again. How are we supposed to deal with her?" As an

orderly wheeled me to the elevator and we moved upward, the only thing that kept me from passing out was the realization that this was the day I was to see Arlene.

I was taken to the same room where the two therapists had stretched my arms and legs a month before. When I realized this, something in me collapsed. Had Arlene lied to me? As I wondered this, I let loose a deep wail, producing a slight whine. *If she did*, I thought, *I'll never trust anyone again.*

The orderly wheeled me into the large room, where a few people had gathered. I thought they were going to untie me from the chair, roll me onto one of the low tables, and start twisting my body again. I started to cry so hysterically that the people stopped talking. The room became quiet.

I was thinking, *Where is Arlene?* Because I didn't see her, I became even more hysterical. As on the day they'd wheeled me into the hall, I tried to wiggle down in the chair. I felt the sheets loosen around my feet and waist, and then my matchstick arms. I raised my head as high as I could. I kept arching back in the chair, thinking that if I moved enough, they wouldn't be able to grab hold of me. My neck felt as taut as the rope we used to swing from over Hook Creek, and as I tossed my head forward, making the room spin around me, Arlene's face came into view.

While I'd been screaming and scooting down in the wheelchair, I hadn't noticed her standing at one end of the room. Now, she was speaking with a dark-haired woman. The two of them approached me. Arlene put her hands on my shoulders.

"It's okay, Julia, we're here to help you," she said, bending down to look me in the eye.

Those words calmed me. Though I didn't quit crying, because of the pain throbbing down my lower back, Arlene's touch and the reassuring tone of her voice convinced me that I was going to be taken care of.

Since my pain was dire, Arlene didn't introduce the dark-haired woman, who was shorter than Arlene and wore a saffron-colored blouse. Her youthful face was framed by her long brown hair. When she spoke, her tone of voice was as kind as Arlene's.

"Could be bedsores," I heard her say.

"Yes," Arlene agreed. "Or it might be the straight-back chair. I don't think her spine can make that low curve."

"I suggest we check for the sores, first," said the dark-haired woman.

Though tears were streaming down my cheeks, I saw Arlene nod. The other woman moved to the front of me, where I could see her face.

"Hello, Julia," she said in a quiet voice, "I'm Joyce Sabari, from occupational therapy. Arlene's told me about you, especially what a fighter you are. I know you're in pain right now, and I'd like to examine your back side, to see if we can determine what's causing the discomfort. Bedsores might be one factor. If so, they should be taken care of right away. Would you let me wheel you into a private room and check you, Julia?"

Her words drew me out of my box of pain. I raised my eyes.

"Good. Let's begin right away."

As she wheeled me to the back of the room, where curtains afforded some privacy, Joyce asked me if I felt a raw pain along my back side. Though it was difficult to differentiate between the general pain needling my every bone and a localized pain, I waited for her to walk around the front of my chair. Then I raised my eyes.

Joyce parted the curtains and wheeled me into a small cubicle. Inside, there was a low table. She closed the curtains behind us.

"I know how hard this must be for you, Julia. You don't even know me, and here I am looking for sores on your back."

She called an assistant who wheeled the Hoyer lift over to us, then helped Joyce untie the sheets and lift me onto the table. Upon being raised out of the chair, I immediately felt less pain. I stopped crying.

"Feels better already, I bet," Joyce said. She brushed a few strands of hair away from my face.

"Next we're going to roll you onto your side, okay?"

I raised my eyes.

After they turned me, Joyce thanked the assistant. She pulled the curtain shut.

"I'm going to be careful, Julia," she said as she put on a pair of rubber gloves. I'm not going to hurt you."

She lifted the blue gown from my back, and I felt the air on my skin as welcome relief.

For a moment, Joyce didn't say anything. I felt her fingers lightly touching my back.

"Oh, my God," she suddenly exclaimed. "These are awful! No wonder you're in pain, Julia. You've got open sores from your middle back all the way down to your thighs."

I imagined the skin rubbed raw, red as Mother's hands washing clothes in cold water on a scrub board.

"Besides being painful," Joyce continued, "these open wounds can lead to other health problems. I recommend that we alert the head nurse and attending physician on your ward. They'll be able to treat you with bedsore medications. But before we do that, I have something for you that might help."

She went out into the main room. When she came back with another therapist, she held a cushion in her hands. I was lifted in the Hoyer. Before I was put back in the wheelchair, Joyce placed the doughnut-shaped cushion on the chair seat.

"This is made of rubber," she informed me. "It's filled with air, like a balloon. I'll tell the nurses to place it beneath you whenever you're in a wheelchair or in your bed. It will alleviate some of the pressure against your skin."

I raised my eyes and then was placed back in the chair with the rubber cushion beneath me. Right away, it helped reduce the pain to the point of tolerance. From this moment on, I held Joyce in highest esteem, right up there with Arlene, who was standing in front of me when the curtains were drawn back.

"Julia is at serious risk of developing decubitus ulcers," Joyce informed her. "I'm going to contact her head nurse right away."

"While you're doing that, I'd like to do something else," Arlene suggested. "Would you mind if I wheel you over to the other side of the room, Julia?"

I looked down.

"Good," she said, as Joyce left the room. "Is it uncomfortable when you look down like that?"

I looked up.

"In that case, why don't we have an understanding that when you'd like to indicate *yes*, continue to look up as you've been doing. When you want to say *no*, simply look straight ahead. Is that agreeable to you?"

I raised my eyes.

"While Joyce is making your appointment, I'd like to do something similar to what we did the other day in your room."

I noticed that people had gathered around me.

"Very well. Now, I'd like to feel your neck and head when you try to nod. May I hold your head gently and feel how much movement you're able to make?"

I looked up.

Arlene moved my head up and down, then from side to side. I felt no pain when she did this. I was able to move the same amount as when she'd been in my room, about three or four inches to the right and two inches to the left.

"Good, Julia. Now try to do that movement by yourself. Try to make a yes movement first."

Almost imperceptibly, I moved my head up and down. Arlene gave me a look of satisfaction. I realized that she'd asked me something no one else had before: to perform a specific action. And I had responded in front of the other people in the room, proving that I understood what Arlene had asked.

I had passed my first test with flying colors. Arlene knew this. When she smiled, a ray of hope stretched across the hole in my heart. With the simple gesture of nodding my head, I broke through the communication barrier.

"Can you lean your head back, so you're looking toward the ceiling?"

I did this and was able to see not only the ceiling, but the general shape of a person standing behind me.

Arlene pondered for a moment. I could tell she had an idea. She looked at me; her face was blank, but I could tell something was going through her mind.

Suddenly, she said, "Look!" and pointed her finger to my left. "Here come your parents!"

What the hell is she talking about, I thought, straining to turn my head. No one was there—just a wall. I looked at her. Either she's crazy or I am. Maybe she's making fun of me.

I felt hurt and a little angry. Arlene was not smiling. Straight-faced, she looked at me. She pointed her finger to my right. "Look at that handsome man!"

When I turned my head to the right, there was nothing but another wall.

I looked at Arlene, and her face expressed sympathy.

She smiled. I realized she'd been testing my ability to understand and respond to directions. I didn't know what the other people's expressions revealed at that moment. Despite the pain, I stopped feeling angry. I was too busy feeling victorious.

Arlene touched my shoulder. "Congratulations, Julia. You did extremely well. I'm sorry I had to do that. Now, I'd like to ask you another question. Would you like to see if the doctors can take the tube out of your nose so you can eat food?"

I raised my eyes so high I practically broke my neck.

"That seems like a pretty solid yes, Julia," Arlene laughed. "I'll see what I can do. One more thing: Would you like to be able to ask questions and let people know what you're thinking?"

I gave her my best affirmative nod.

"Then there's a machine I'd like to show you sometime."

The door to the room opened, and Joyce walked back in.

"It's all set. A doctor will examine Julia's bedsores tomorrow morning."

Arlene nodded. "I was just telling Julia about the Porta Printer."

"Yes," Joyce continued. "After the ulcers are cleared up, we'd like to show you some new equipment. You might even be one of the first to use this communication device."

She said the right thing. I made a mental note that no

matter what obstacles I faced, I'd try whatever these two offered me.

"But first things first," Joyce said, level-headed as always. "Let's get you back to your room and into a comfortable position in bed."

· · ·

Joyce wheeled me out of OT and into the main hall. I felt tremendous gratitude toward both her and Arlene for all they were doing to help me. Problem was, I couldn't give them proper thanks. There was still no way for me to convey my thoughts to others. I could only raise my eyes, trusting that they'd intuit the meaning of thanks in that gesture.

Because of the cushion Joyce had given me, I wasn't in so much pain. I could pay attention to the world around me. I saw my legs out, parallel to the floor, resting in the chair's open foot slats. It was a miracle just to sit up, to move along a corridor where people walked and talked, interacted, exchanged nods, smiled and laughed, cajoled, and called each other by their first names. So not all the people here are mute or crazy, I thought. Nor are they completely paralyzed.

What a pleasure it was to move through space, to feel air on my face, to be upright, aware, looking at the gorgeous man turning the wheels of his chair with arms big enough to wrap around a tree. A black woman with a quilt covering the stubs where her legs used to be reminded me of Mrs.

Anderson back on John Street. Her quilt made me think of the blankets my sister Midge used to stitch for relatives at Christmas.

"A lot of people came to Goldwater because of various forms of congenital diseases—cerebral palsy, muscular dystrophy—and some are here because of problems that strike later, like multiple sclerosis and Alzheimer's," explained Joyce. "Still others had various accidents—gunshot wounds, car wrecks—nasty things like that. And others, like yourself, had strokes."

Though I still didn't know exactly what that word *stroke* meant, I related it to what my mother had said that day so long ago—*hemorrhage*—and I figured it had to do with bleeding in my brain. Yet I could think clearly. I wondered why.

All the way back to the ward, the world seemed rightside up for the first time since I'd come out of the coma. I looked at the different wheelchairs people were maneuvering through the halls. Some were made of metal, some of wood. One small blonde woman propelled her chair forward with her arms. As we passed her, I turned my head.

"Hello, Ann," Joyce said. The woman looked at Joyce and smiled. Then she propelled her chair past us.

"It's now thought that Ann and people in her predicament will soon be able to use special devices to move around. Imagine going outside on sunny days and not telling anyone. That's possible. But only if you have a wheelchair. I know it sounds crazy to you, but I've recently learned of a wheelchair that can be operated by pressing a switch. Now that you have proven that you can move your head, Arlene and I may be able to adapt a single switch for you. If you can use it, there's a possibility you'll be able to control a motorized wheelchair."

I thought of my blue car and realized that Joyce was right: a wheelchair might be the only way for me to move around. Not like four-on-the-floor, but movement all the same. The one thing that made me hesitate was the pain I'd felt every time I'd been in one. How would Joyce be able to find a wheelchair that I could sit in comfortably for those jaunts outside?

"If nothing else, you'll get to see the ward you're on and what's beyond the four walls of your room."

For the rest of the ride back, I imagined sitting in my own chair, leaving the hospital for the sun near the river, discovering where I was and what place I'd have here.

As we crossed the threshold to the D ward, two nurses stopped talking. I looked them square in the face.

"Hello," Joyce said. "Ms. Tavalaro has a new cushion beneath her. Would you place it under her at all times? It will help her posterior ulcers heal."

The nurses looked at me and nodded.

"And would you mind putting Julia back into bed? Don't want the wheelchair to exacerbate those sores."

She looked at me and smiled. "See you soon, Julia."

I raised my eyes, in joy.

Chapter Ten

FACE IN THE MIRROR

I found myself floating
On the half-frozen waters
Of a fabulous sea, drifting
Up & down
Down & up
Until

I sunk
To the ocean floor.
Suddenly
Above me, the frozen waters
Were ringed in fire
Yes fire
T'was encircling me
Hot vapors burned my skin
I screamed in protest
The frozen waters
Became the torturing Red
Red waters of the sea

I looked up
& saw me.

Within a week from when I first met Joyce, someone came to my room and tacked a sign over my bed:

Julia Tavalaro Understands Everything You Say.

I thought that my life would change then, that people would stop mistreating me. I also believed that someone from the hospital would alert my family to the good news and that they'd come back to see me. I wondered how old Judy was, guessing close to eight. I wondered how my mother and father were getting along and imagined how glad they'd be to know I understood what was going on around me. Though it seemed futile, I still hoped they'd come and take me home.

Though I waited anxiously each day for them to appear, it wasn't until three weeks after the sign was hung over my bed that anyone in my family came to visit. My mother came alone, dressed in pink and carrying a white purse. Her hair was untidy and she looked distraught. She slipped quietly into my room, and came over to my bed.

"My baby," she said, "my precious girl. Me and Joanie both knew you were awake all this time. Like a woman knowing she's pregnant, I knew without asking any doctors. O moj boze, I knew, but couldn't do anything."

She brushed her gray hair out of her eyes, and wiped a tear from her cheek.

"You must forgive me, my precious girl. And your father. We've hardly had a night's sleep since you went unconscious. I've prayed night and day for God to protect you and keep you safe. That's all I could do, Julie."

She reached down then and touched my cheek. Then she leaned over and rested her face against mine, and I couldn't keep from crying. When she let go of my shoulders and raised her face, I could see her wet cheeks and my own tears staining her dress. I wanted her to tell me how Judy was, and when she would be able to take me home. But after she stood up, her hands opening and closing nervously at her side, she only said that she'd been trying to get George to bring Judy to visit.

"But that man, I tell you! He won't even mention your name to that little girl. I'm afraid she's going to grow up thinking that Mae is her real mother."

Though I was used to the heat of anger rising up in me, I thought my head would explode with rage when my mother told me this. I wanted to get out of bed more than ever, rush home, and take Judy away from her father. I wanted to hold her and tell her that I'd always love her, no matter what condition I was in. Yet I still had no way to tell my mother these things. Nor did I have any way to vent the anger that had been building in me all these years, threatening my sanity.

Once more, Mother reached her hand down to my

face and cupped her palm around my cheek. "I love you, Julie." Then, as if she couldn't face the pain of my condition, she went to the window and looked out. Moments passed before she turned back to me. I thought she would get a chair and sit for a while beside my bed, but she held her purse in the inner crook of her elbow, walked back, and, looking down at me, said she couldn't stay long but she'd be back soon. "I'll try to bring Judy," she said, bending down to kiss me on the forehead. "I'll try."

My mother's visit made me very angry. Here I had just been discovered as cognitive, and she couldn't even stay long enough to tell me how everyone in my family was. She didn't think about what I might have wanted to know, such as Judy's age, or how Joanie was doing; nor did she tell me who had contacted her about my condition, though I reasoned it had most likely been Arlene. Mother seemed burdened by a guilt that weighed so heavily on her that she couldn't bear to occupy my room for any length of time. What should have been a celebration, with all of my family members attending—from George and Judy on down to Joanie's small children—turned sour. Even after everyone knew I was a thinking human being, my family continued to ignore me. I felt that their reaction to the news of my cognizance was to leave me lying in bed, isolated, alone, craving companionship.

I'd like to say that my caregivers came rushing to my bedside and began treating me with dignity. But that was not the case, either. Though they noted that I was aware of what was transpiring around me, the quality of my care didn't change much in those first few months after Arlene's discovery. In some ways it became even worse, which makes me wonder if they really wanted me to be cognitive at all.

One of the good things that happened after the sign was put above my bed was that a doctor and a nurse came to my room one day to remove the tube in my throat. As they walked over to me, the doctor was questioning the nurse. "Have you noticed any change in this patient's behavior?"

"No," the nurse replied, "same as always. But speech did send someone to see her a while back—you know, the tall one. And then they recently took her up to OT, and another therapist brought her back. She gave us a butterfly cushion to put under her when she's in bed. They think she's cognitive."

"They're requesting removal of the nasogastric tube," the doctor interjected. "They say the patient asked to have it taken out."

"I seriously doubt that, seeing she can't even talk. And how's she gonna eat? She's already livin' on nothin' but liquid."

"They believe she's reacting appropriately to environmental stimulus."

The nurse looked down at me. She bent over and waved her open hand in front of my face. "Look at her," she said to the doctor, "does that look like the face of some-body thinkin'?"

The doctor shrugged. "Speech says she responds with eye movements."

The nurse stopped moving her hand and backed away from my bed. She looked at the wall and saw the sign.

" 'Julia Tavalaro understands everything you say,' " she read out loud. "Who put that there?"

The doctor looked up at the sign. He walked quickly around the bed and reached for the tube in my left nostril. He jiggled it, as if testing how easily it would slip out. I had almost forgotten what breathing would be like without it, and how it would feel to eat food again.

"Get me some alcohol," he told the nurse, who left the room and came back with a plastic bottle. She moistened a piece of cotton with the alcohol and stood beside the doc-tor as he pulled the tube from my nose. When it came out, I felt momentary pain, followed by welcome relief and a burst of joy.

"She'll have to go on a semisolid soft diet," the doctor said. "Avoid clear liquids to prevent aspiration. Meds should be mixed with semisolids—applesauce or pudding."

"And I suppose I have to be the one to start her off, huh?"

"I guess it's your lucky day. I'm going to the A ward. Be back this afternoon to check on her."

After the doctor left, I wondered what the A ward was. Since I'd never been to the A ward, I thought it might be for people who were partially functional. If so, people living there might have more independence. Now that I was officially cognitive, I wanted to explore the possibility of moving there.

The nurse raised my bed and positioned me upright. She arranged a sheet flat against my chest and wrapped it around my neck. Out of fear, I started to cry; the sheet still reminded me of the day they tied me into a wheelchair. "Whachu cryin' 'bout, girl. Who do you think you are, anyway, Queen Bee?" She looked me full in the face. "So you understand, huh? Well, if you're so smart, where you at now?" She pointed one finger toward the ceiling. "You died and gone to heaven or what?" she demanded, finger pointed stiffly up.

I looked toward the direction of her finger, thinking what a stupid question. She opened a tray on the table beside my bed, and as I smelled the pungent odor of something like stuffed cabbage, Joyce walked in.

"Hello, Julia. How are you today?" She carried a small white bowl. I looked at her, then over at the nurse.

"I see you've had the tube removed. Bet that feels a lot better. And," she said, looking up at the wall behind my bed, "someone's put your sign up."

The nurse's mouth had fallen open.

"You mean to tell me she understands what you're saying?"

"Yes, ma'am," Joyce replied. "According to speech therapy and OT, it seems true that Ms. Tavalaro understands what's going on around her."

"Well, I'll be . . ." the nurse whispered under her breath. "We all thought she was brain dead."

"Apparently that's not true," Joyce countered. "Ms. Tavalaro understands and, hopefully, will one day be able to communicate with you."

"Communicate? You mean talk?" the nurse asked, raising her eyebrows.

"Speech is still evaluating Julia to see if she has potential to use a device to type out what she wants to say. For now, she raises her eyes to indicate a positive response to questions. Don't you, Julia?"

I looked at the nurse and raised my eyes as high as I could.

"Well, I'll be . . . I had no idea. Neither do any of the other aides." She went to the door, shaking her head. "I'm gonna go tell the others." She turned in the doorway for one last look at me. "I'll be . . ."

Joyce took the nurse's chair and sat down beside me. "I guess that's the first anyone knew you're aware."

I raised my eyes.

"Must feel like quite a personal victory for you."

I looked up, emphatically.

"I brought you something. Do you like Jell-O? It's raspberry."

I smiled inside, thinking how Mom used to say that Jell-O was the easiest dessert in the world to make.

"Like to try some? I brought you a spoon."

I raised my eyes, and thought about how many times I'd craved my favorite foods since I'd woken up from the

coma. I wanted solid food so badly that I'd be lying in bed
trying to go to sleep, when I'd imagine a linen-covered ta-
blecloth set with china plates piled high with food: one just
for fruit—ripe oranges, peaches, pears, plums, and cherries;
one with Romaine lettuce and the cheeses that used to make
my mouth water—cheddar, Roquefort, Parmesan, and
Swiss; a platter of macaroni and cheese beside the one
overflowing with pasta and tomato sauce. Of course there
was no meat, but I did manage to arrange for an assortment
of baked fish, lobster with lots of butter, and a tureen of
clams and mussels. And I didn't skimp on the desserts, especially strawberry shortcake and German chocolate cake.
Finally, at the end of the table was a silver tray of Godiva
chocolates.

During those nights when I lay dreaming of food, I
felt as if I was stranded, parched and famished, in the desert.
And now, as Joyce pulled the sheet to my chin, I was back
in civilization, being fed by this kind woman who'd
surprised me with Jell-O. Though Jell-O wasn't on my list
of delicacies, I was happy to watch Joyce mash it with the
spoon and then place a small bite in my mouth. It was a
cool shock of flavor that burst against my palate. I savored
the sweet taste of raspberry fruit, as if that simple dessert
were an exotic delicacy from halfway around the world.

"How's that?" Joyce asked.

I raised my eyes and smiled at the thought that I was
eating food again for the first time in more than six years.

"Do you mind if I talk to you while you eat?"

I looked straight ahead for *no.*

"I'd like to fill you in on some details of the plan Arlene and I are devising for your therapies. I think it's important to give you as much control as possible."

I watched her spoon more Jell-O into my mouth. Until that moment, I'd not considered that I'd ever be able to control anything again in my life.

"First of all, do you know what occupational therapy is?"

I looked straight ahead.

"For starters, it's about what all of us—you, Arlene, the nursing staff, and myself—can do together to improve the quality of your life. Even if you can only move your neck and eyes, you're still *able* to think for yourself."

She paused, looking out the window at the sun streaming through. I wondered if I'd ever be able to do anything for myself.

"Unseasonably warm for this early in spring, especially after such a bad winter. How's the Jell-O going down? Do you feel any difficulty swallowing?"

I looked straight ahead. Though I had to eat very slowly, I felt satisfied. I was, after all, eating without a machine grinding beside me. Yet my mouth and throat felt strange, the way I used to feel after having cavities filled at the dentist's office. Though my facial muscles didn't feel numb, I couldn't control them enough to keep all the food in my mouth.

"My job is to determine which tasks of daily living—

and by that I mean feeding, washing, ambulating—you can accomplish with minimal assistance. I don't want to give you false hope in terms of being able to walk again. And we don't know about vocalizing. You may indeed be able to produce louder sounds if the tube in your throat is removed. One thing is certain: you have the ability to move your neck. That's crucial. The next step is for you to learn how to control that movement so you can hit a switch."

She paused. Sun struck the red flowers on her pink blouse, and I remembered my favorite scarf, the one with the blue daisies. More than ever, I wanted my old clothes back.

"Once we determine if you're capable of using a switch, Arlene and I will work with you to set up an individualized program." She placed the bowl on the bedside table, then pressed her left palm against her cheek. "We'll work with what you *can* do, no matter how seemingly insignificant."

She leaned closer to me. "Once we determine if you can indeed use your neck and head movements to operate a switch, we can start testing various wheelchairs. Fortunately, Goldwater has an excellent technical staff. Plus, you're right on the cutting edge of a new revolution in power wheelchairs. This hospital is probably the best place in the country right now for getting you into a motorized chair."

Joyce stopped spooning the Jell-O. We sat in silence for a moment.

"Because you've been lying still for so long, your range of motion is greatly limited," she continued. "Every day, someone should have been moving your arms and legs for you. That way, your limbs wouldn't be so constricted. To prevent this, you should have had someone moving your limbs every day. Often, the family does this."

I started to cry. I thought of Joan telling me that she and Mom used to move my arms. Yet years had passed since then.

"The good part is that there's a lot of new equipment here at Goldwater. Exercises can also help reduce muscle tension."

Through my tears, I wondered how my hands and arms could get any tighter. My forearms were already contracted against my chest, causing my shoulders to ache. My legs were whittled slivers of bone bending inward at each foot.

"Arlene and I have come up with a preliminary plan, in two parts. First thing is to get you out of bed and into a wheelchair. I'll take care of this. Then we'd like to create a way for you to communicate with those around you. Arlene will design your communication program. Ultimately, we'd like to use the latest technology for both objectives— finding a wheelchair you'll be able to control without assistance, and enabling you to write messages to those around you, including the nurses and other people on the ward."

If Joyce hadn't been looking at me with a dead-serious expression, I'd have laughed or cried, or both at once. Instead, I looked at her and saw a bronze-colored watch on her wrist.

Time ticked. I raised my eyes in hope.

. . .

Not long after Joyce's visit, I was granted a welcome surprise. My mother brought Judy and two of George's nieces to visit. Judy, who must have been eight or so, had long bangs and was so tall and grown-up that I hardly recognized her. She wore a dark blue sweater with white sleeves and a blue skirt. She had a wide, mischievous smile and dark-brown, shoulder-length hair. I could still recognize the face of the baby I'd held back on Roosevelt Street. But there was another face there, that of a budding girl I couldn't be so sure I knew.

Mom wore a blue and white sleeveless dress. It was a warm spring day, and the first thing she did was open the window. I saw how her arms had gotten bigger, her hands mapped in wrinkles. When she opened the window, her neck muscles tightened, and I saw the familiar determined strain in her face. Though she smiled when she looked at me, I saw sorrow in the lines around her mouth, pity in her blue-gray eyes.

George's nieces, Linda and Barbara, must have been in their teens. They looked as uncomfortable to be here as Mom and Judy did. In between shuffling their feet and throwing sidelong glances into the corridor, they told me they'd heard I could use my eyes to communicate. I smiled and raised my eyes. If I could have spoken, I would have told them how grateful I was for Arlene's intervention, for her realizing I was alive inside.

"To celebrate," Linda said, "we've brought some goodies." She held up a grocery sack and started pulling things out. "Here's a couple of nightgowns that my mom's opened at the back so the nurses can dress you easier. A pink one and a blue one, Aunt Julie." She held the pink one up against her body.

"And here's some makeup!" she continued, laying the nightgown at the foot of my bed. "We thought you might like Barb and me to do your face." She held up a compact.

I looked at my mother, and she leaned over, touching her cheek to mine. Grinning from ear to ear, Judy glanced at me. I thought how nice it would be for her to see me dressed up, my face with some color painted onto it. It might even soothe her to see me made up like other women.

"And here's lipstick," Barbara said, digging into the bottom of the bag.

"And some rouge and eyeliner," Linda added. "Best of all, we brought you a blonde wig."

She raised the wig into the air. A part of me wanted nothing more than to be treated to my old pleasures. I tried not to think how much I missed using makeup and going out in nice dresses. Another part of me wanted to spit at the whole thing.

"We thought we could dress you up," Barbara said,

"and take some pictures. Wouldn't that be fun, Aunt Julie?"

Mom opened her purse and took something out. She leaned over me and taped a picture of Jesus to my bedpost. She didn't say anything, maybe out of guilt for not having been able to visit me more than once a month since I'd awakened from the coma. I knew she probably couldn't have afforded more frequent trips to the hospital.

"Want to try the wig, Aunt Julie?" Barbara implored.

I hesitated. A blonde wig and four visitors. Could be worse, I thought. I could be sitting here unable to respond.

"C'mon, Aunt Julie!" Linda pleaded. "We just want to have some fun and brighten your day a little. Look, I brought light-pink lipstick, the kind people said you used to like. And here's some pale eye shadow. I even remembered to bring a mirror."

She reached back into the bag and held up a portable mirror. It was round and had a wire stand hinged at the back. Linda stood it up on the table beside me. It reflected bits of light and parts of the room. I saw the ceiling lights and a shimmer off the window. Then Linda moved the mirror, and I saw myself.

For a second, I didn't think it was me. It was a shock to see my dark-brown hair, once thick and bleached blonde, now tangled and unkempt. Much of it had fallen out. I could see streaks of my fair-skinned scalp. The skin of my face sagged, and lines were embedded across my once-smooth forehead. My lips, once full of color, were now pale and undefined. Near my jaw, I caught a hint of an emaciated hand, which appeared to be thin joints of bone covered in flesh so pale it seemed transparent.

"Okay, Aunt Julie, I'll leave it up to you. Decide for yourself."

Mom went to the window. I looked at her and smelled damp earth, the hint of something blooming. I couldn't keep from looking back into the mirror. It was the strangest feeling to look at myself and not recognize who I was. I wanted to cry and toss the mirror through the window, but I realized that this would be senseless. Somehow, I had to accept who I was now.

My face began to contort and lengthen as I started to cry. Judy stepped back farther from the bed. She looked like she didn't know what to expect from me, as if I could do damage at any second.

After a moment I thought, What the hell. I haven't done anything fun for over six years. Here Linda and Barbara had bothered to bring this stuff to cheer me up. I couldn't turn them down—it would be ungrateful, not to mention impolite. Their faces were bright and shining, as if they were expecting me to get up and walk or perform some other impossible task. My face softened, and Judy moved toward the bed. I looked at Barbara and raised my eyes.

"Linda, she said yes. Look!"

Linda looked at me, and I raised my eyes again.

My nieces went into action. They stood on either side of me. Linda held the mirror, while Barbara put on the foundation, the blush, and the eye shadow. Then they switched. Linda leaned over me with the eyebrow pencil. I looked in the mirror and lowered my eyes so she could line the bottom lid.

"Barb, she knows when to look down!"

I looked down again. She leaned close enough for me to see the makeup on her own face.

"She knows when to close her eyes for me to apply the eye makeup."

I felt the mascara being curled on.

"Look, Barb. She knows when to move her head."

Mom pulled the chair over and sat down beside me. "I knew it, Julie, and so did Joanie. You could hear me during those visits, those times I sat near your bed and talked. Joanie and me knew. We both knew. But nobody would listen to us. And God knows I couldn't make the trip more. Fifteen dollars each time for the transportation alone."

I knew it was brave of my mother to speak to me like this. It crossed my mind that it was probably because she and Joan had told the hospital staff I was awake that they decided to give me therapy. That might have been why I was taken to OT the first time. I realized how difficult it must be for a parent to lose her daughter in the prime of life. But I was angry that she and Joan had given up on me when the hospital still thought I wasn't aware and that no one but Mom had bothered to visit as soon as I was known to be cognitive. If the roles had been reversed, I would have kept the pressure on until someone knew I was serious.

Within forty-five minutes they had a new pink gown

on me and enough gunk on my face to make a whore drop dead. The wig felt awful, like dog hair with lining. Yet, I had a ball remembering the times Mrs. Anderson used to give us makeup and Joanie and I would sneak upstairs and put it on in front of Mom's mirror.

"If your father could see you now!" Mom said, looking at me from the foot of my bed.

I smiled at her.

Barbara held the mirror in front of me so I could have a long look. I couldn't believe what I saw. Even all gussied up, I didn't know the person in the mirror. If I had known her, I'd have felt sorry for her. She was skin and bones, a few teeth, some sagging flesh, and fake color. Her hands were like a baby's, always held in a fist. Her head lolled from side to side, and the wig looked awful. I had no idea how much I'd aged in six years. Instead of Judy's mother, I could have been her grandmother.

"Aunt Julie, we have something else for you," Linda said.

She held up an Instamatic camera, and I thought of how I used to love to have my picture taken. Though I had never been certain about my father's erratic behavior or my mother's reaction to him, I could always be sure of my looks when I was a young woman. Suddenly I detected a part of that woman in me.

"C'mon, Judy, go stand by your mother," Linda suggested.

Judy came over and stood to the right of my bed. She

put her hand near my head, and I wondered who would teach her about becoming a woman.

Mom came over and stood on the opposite side of the bed.

Linda flashed a photo. Suddenly, I felt good about doing this. At least there would be proof of the three generations spanned by my mother, myself, and Judy.

Barbara put the mirror back into the bag, and as a man brought dinner trays into the room, the three of them said good-bye. As they left, Judy looked back at me. Barbara and Linda waved. Mom blew me a kiss. Silently, I thanked them from the bottom of my heart.

Chapter Eleven

POEM IN MIND

Take this poem home
Read it no feed it to the mind
The mind fabulously famished
The mind oh so hungry
Please
Take the poem home
Feed it to the mind
Poem in mind.

Not long after my mother and nieces visited, I was positioned in a new wheelchair and taken once more to occupational therapy. The blue chair had a sloping back. If I was positioned properly, I could sit for prolonged periods. My bedsores were nearly healed, and I wasn't feeling as much pain as when I'd first met Joyce.

"This band," she informed me, snapping it to my head, "is designed to hold a curved metal rod. It will help you point to letters on a typewriter. I'm also hoping that the pointer will make it possible for you to turn the pages of a book. Like to try it on, Julia?"

It'd be good for poking someone's eye out, I thought.

Joyce rested her hands lightly on my shoulders. I looked at her, unsure how I'd ever be able to point or read. Yet she was so encouraging that I raised my eyes, in determination.

"I want to emphasize that this is not always going to be easy. There might be days when you'll get so frustrated you'll want to quit. But this is a good device to use, at first, because it starts working your neck muscles. The more you can turn your head, the greater the chances that you'll be able to operate a switch. If you can use a switch, you might be a candidate for a motorized wheelchair."

She slipped the metal rod into the front of the headband. "Can you point to the letter *J?*

I leaned forward. I saw *J* clearly and tried to strike the letter. But I couldn't coordinate my head motion, the length of the pointer, and the keyboard in front of me. I missed the key.

"Good," Joyce said. "You're able to make contact with the keyboard. Don't be hard on yourself. Just try again."

No matter how hard I tried that day, my chin wouldn't tuck, and my neck wouldn't extend enough. I couldn't strike the letter *J.*

. . .

The same week that Joyce fitted me with the headstick pointer, I was taken to see Arlene in speech therapy. The day was overcast. When Arlene stood up to greet me, I saw a sky full of heavy, dark clouds in the window behind her.

"I've made a letter board for you, Julia," she began, holding up a piece of plywood with the alphabet painted across it. Even though I didn't know how I'd use it, I smiled.

"Joyce tells me you've had your first session with the headstick pointer," she said. "I hope you'll be able to use it with this board. I think it'll prove easier than hitting those typewriter keys. You just point to the letters and spell words."

I thought of how I'd always disliked spelling. In school, I was never very good at it. Though I loved the sound of words, I'd always thought they were to be spoken instead of read. Now, I had no choice but to spell things out, letter by letter.

"Like to try?"

I raised my eyes, and she held the board out in front of me.

I pointed to *W*.

"Is the letter *W*, Julia?"

I raised my eyes.

I looked at *H* and remembered the way I used to close my left eye to aim down the length of one of Dad's guns. I had to compress space like I did back then, imagining the letter *H* to be a duck. I aimed and struck it with the pointer. This continued until I spelled, W-H-E-N W-I-L-L I S-P-E-A-K A-G-A-I-N.

Arlene lowered the board and looked at me. "I don't know the answer to that question, Julia. It's possible that the strokes did not completely destroy your vocal system. But we won't know for sure until the cannula tube's taken out. After it's removed, some people do regain their ability to speak. Others can still only emit incoherent sounds. Problem is, we still don't know if you have any control of the muscles around your vocal chords. We won't know what sounds you'll be able to produce until we try to strengthen your mouth muscles with therapy."

I looked at the board, and Arlene held it up again.

"Like to spell something else?" she asked.

W-H-E-N C-A-N I-T B-E T-A-K-E-N O-U-T.

"That I don't know," she offered, putting the board on her desk and opening a file folder. "I've been looking into it. What I've found is that your medical history has been a rocky one. At one point since you've been in the hospital, you weighed only seventy-four and a half pounds. You've lived through three serious clashes with pneumonia and more than one brush with death."

She closed the folder and reached for the letter board. "Because of your history of respiratory infection, the doctors may want to keep the tube in. But now, with your new diet and the exercise you'll get from attending speech and OT activities, your health might improve."

I raised my eyes and looked at the board: W-H-A-T Y-E-A-R I-S I-T.

"It's 1974, Julia."

I started to spell J-U-D-Y, but I got choked up. A tear tipped onto my hospital gown. I wondered how much longer I'd have to wear these clothes.

"Like to talk about your daughter?"

I started to raise my eyes, but then changed my mind. I suddenly realized that I'd lost Judy for good. She'd never be able to treat me like a human being, let alone her own mother. If I was ever to be happy again, I'd have to accept the fact that Judy would never be a large part of my life. I'd have to be content to live with memories of her.

I looked over at the window. The clouds were breaking up, causing a curtain of light to fall to the ground. The room brightened. Arlene saw me looking out the window. She turned toward it, and the sun lit up the sky. A rainbow, caused by a heavy downpour off in the distance, formed in the east.

"Isn't that beautiful?" Arlene asked, looking over at me.

I raised my eyes.

"Do you mind if I open the window?"

I looked straight at her, "no." As I felt a soft breeze blow into the room, I realized that instead of talking about Judy, I wanted to mention something that would make me feel good.

I faced the letter board and spelled, I W-A-N-T M-Y C-L-O-T-H-E-S B-A-C-K.

"Don't blame you one bit. I would, too. Who do you think could help get them?"

"S-I-S-T-E-R J-O-A-N A-N-D M-O-M."

"I'll see if I can contact your mother and sister. Maybe they'll be able to bring in some of your things. If not, we'll think of something else. How's that sound?"

I raised my eyes and flashed her my best smile. Though it was not adequate compensation for all she was doing for me, it was the only way, besides spelling, that I could thank her.

"You got it. Another important item to discuss is increasing your degree of head motion," she informed me, looking closely at my neck and shoulders. "I see you're able to move your head some to use the pointer. That movement in itself opens up communication possibilities. What I'd like to do is focus on side-to-side movement."

She demonstrated by turning her head slowly, left to right. "This movement is crucial for activating a switch. Joyce told me that she mentioned the motorized wheelchair to you. If you can turn your head and apply enough pressure, you might be able to operate not only a wheelchair but a communication device."

Though I didn't know exactly what she meant, it sounded hopeful. I raised my eyes.

"Main thing is to be flexible. There's going to be a lot of trial and error before we can determine what you're capable of using."

I looked at the letter board.

Arlene held it up while I spelled, T-H-A-N-K U
F-O-R H-E-L-P.

She nodded. "It's my pleasure. It's also my job. I was
hired to help people like you."

W-H-E-N D-O W-E S-T-A-R-T.

"I knew from the beginning you were a go-getter. Let's
start right away."

. . .

During the next two years, I continued practicing head and
neck movements, spelling words on various letter boards,
and typing (which I hated and soon gave up). Some days,
I'd spend the afternoon reading in the hospital's library,
where Joyce had arranged for a rack to be set up in front of
my wheelchair. The librarian would play a tape of the book
I wanted to read, while I followed along, using the headstick pointer to turn the pages. I especially enjoyed murder mysteries, like *Murder on the Orient Express*, by Agatha
Christie.

Despite the pleasure of reading, it became evident that
the head pointer would not be ideal for communicating.
Every time I wore it, I had the terrible feeling that because
of the pressure it caused, I'd get a headache and experience
another stroke. Though I knew the fear was unfounded, I
nonetheless became frightened, even panic-stricken, if anything caused pressure against my head.

As an alternative, Joyce strapped a light to my head,

enabling me to direct its beam onto a grid containing the alphabet. After I pointed the light at a specific letter, it would be printed on a thin strip of paper resembling ticker tape. This optical head-pointer system would have been a good way for me to communicate, except that it, too, caused the same fear as the headstick pointer. Also, someone had to be on hand to cut the strips of paper when I finished writing. Even though I was soon spending four to five hours a day in the speech and OT offices, it wasn't always possible for someone to take time away from other patients, some of whom were going through experiences as dire as my own.

Arlene thought that a switch would solve these problems. During one speech session, she used Velcro to attach a switch at the height of my right cheek. She placed a detachable table over the wheelchair arms, and she arranged the ticker-tape printer in front of me. Instead of pointing a light to the letter I wanted, I simply had to watch as the machine lit up the letters, one by one. When it reached the letter I wanted, I turned my head to the right and leaned against the switch, and the letter was printed.

After I demonstrated that I could use the switch, Arlene tested me on five different writing devices. Some were floor models. Others were small enough to be placed on a special table laid over my bed. The best one was a Macintosh computer Arlene set up in the solarium, down the hall from my room. It was on this device that I wrote my first poem:

ANGER

I can see it in the eyes of animals,
Man and us.
We get aggravated, frustrated, intimidated,
But for what?
People who know me well
Say that I've built a powerful shell.
Through years, with fears, in tears
I have patiently waited
To be deceased
And for the new world
To begin.

When I finished this poem and saw it printed, I felt I had achieved a miracle. After more than six years of lying immobile, followed by two years of intensive training, I could finally communicate in the voice I'd been hearing in my head.

"Anger" was my attempt to express the feelings that my sister Midge, my mother, and I had in common: that we couldn't get along romantically with men. Apparently, other people had the same feeling, for one day this poem was read in the auditorium, as a farewell to the hospital's director. Afterward, the director congratulated me, making me realize that I could contribute to the lives of other people.

I determined to write even more. If I wasn't in speech therapy or OT, or fighting my latest battle with the nurses,

I'd be in front of the Macintosh. That grid of letters became so burned into my mind that wherever I looked—a nurse's face, a spoonful of pureed potatoes, a woman's stone-cold expression as she stared at a wall—letters appeared.

One of the subjects I wrote about was love. As I lay in bed one day, I contemplated why both of my marriages had failed. Jim and I had been so obsessed—he with his weight lifting and me with my desire to have a family—that we hardly noticed one another. We rarely even listened to what the other person had to say. As for George, I think I'd seen him as a provider and as a man with whom to have children. He gave me possessions galore—the house, the furniture, money—as well as a beautiful daughter and the two foster children. But there was something about being close to another person that terrified us. We both built walls around our emotions. While writing one day, I had a realization. My upbringing had left me craving to be cared for. Mom and Dad never had enough of anything—food, clothes, doctors' care—and in marrying George, I had found safety. I used my writing to explore some of these ideas, plus the fact of there being no one to blame for my misfortune.

Here's another poem, written the same week as "Anger":

BROKEN HEARTS
Broken hearts are torn in two
One for me and one for you.

No more bodies held together
So you can hear their heart beat call.
No more kisses of exotic ecstasy
Thrown into eternity. No more
Hands clasped, as if
We're one
So that no more ice, water, or oceans
Can come between us.
Tell me, good God, who is to blame?
Is it he or she, perhaps both?
No name to call such shame.
No name.

In the middle of writing "Broken Hearts," I realized that the act of creating poetry was now the most important way for me to communicate. But how would I have the patience to complete each letter, each message, each poem? How would I find a quiet place in the hospital where I could work in concentration? And could my words help me break out of this implacable silence?

I found part of the answer to these questions in rhyme. I started hearing the rhyme in people's everyday speech. I focused on the sounds of language and soon discovered that I could use rhyme to remember lines. I'd hear a line in my mind, then find rhymes to help me complete the poem. By the time I got to the Macintosh, I'd have memorized the whole poem.

I started thinking in terms of words, translating objects into their corresponding letters. Even when I slept, I dreamed I was crawling over the alphabet, my body small as a baby's. The letters formed a children's playground. The long, slanting legs of the letter *A* were dual slides I careened down, touching the ground with my bare feet. I ran to *O* in the shape of a Ferris wheel, like the one Father had taken me to at Coney Island when I was a little girl. *H* was the haunted house at Halloween; *X*, the skull and crossbones forbidding entrance to the *SSS*nakepit where I might be eaten alive. *M* was the tidal wave I floated on; *S*, the swift cutting of a crosscurrent; *U*, the deep dive down; *V*, the steep swoop up. *J* stood for my name. Hearing my name, I woke up, happy to be alive, sad to be silent, grateful to hear an unfamiliar voice near me.

The voice was clear. I thought I heard a note of sympathy in its tone. I opened my eyes and saw a tall man standing near my bed. "Julia, I'm sorry to wake you. My name's Jim Crawford. I'm a psychologist here at the hospital. Arlene suggested I come speak to you."

. . .

In the late summer of 1976, I was taken to my first appointment with Dr. Crawford. Because his name was the same as my first husband's, from the start I took to addressing him more formally than I had my other caregivers. He was a neat dresser—carefully creased dark slacks, a blue tie, and a blue and white plaid shirt. He wore glasses and had a head of thick, curly hair. He positioned my wheelchair directly in front of his desk. His voice was gentle, yet determined.

"Arlene has given me an alphabet card to use in our work together."

He held up a plastic board the size of a piece of writing paper. I saw the alphabet printed in neat rows, five letters across and six rows down.

"I'll hold the card and point to the letters. When I get to the letter that forms part of the word you'd like to spell, raise your eyes. That way, you can spell out words and sentences. I'll respond to those."

I raised my eyes to indicate that I understood.

"Let's start with your wheelchair," Dr. Crawford began. "Though that's OT's department, I'd like to ask if you'd care to ambulate in a motorized chair?"

I remembered Joyce telling me that a switch might enable me to drive a wheelchair. In response to Dr. Crawford's question, I raised my eyes. H-O-W C-A-N I D-R-I-V-E M-O-T-O-R-I-Z-E-D C-H-A-I-R, I spelled.

"Good question. As you know, Arlene thinks you're fully functional with the head switch. Since you're able to use it to write with, you're probably ready to give it a go on a wheelchair. The mechanics in the wheelchair shop may be able to customize a chair for you, hooking it to the new electronic scanning device."

I looked at him, remembering what Arlene had told me a few weeks before. She'd spoken with a friend of hers at Children's Hospital in Stanford, California. They had a technician who had created a special scanning device. "Basically," Arlene had said, "it's a small electronic device that can be mounted above your wheelchair. When you sit in the chair, you'll see a red light flashing around a dial. The dial shows directions—forward, left, right, reverse—and when the light flashes in the direction you wish to go, you press a switch. This activates the wheelchair's electrical mechanism."

With Dr. Crawford continuing to speak in front of me, I began piecing things together. I raised my eyes, thinking how I'd love to move again instead of being pushed around like a piece of dead wood. I wanted to challenge my circumstances and learn to move myself.

"I take it you're raising your eyes to tell me you'd like to try the wheelchair?"

I raised my eyes again.

"I'll let OT know your wishes. They'll take it from there. Undoubtedly, this wheelchair system will improve your self-esteem. You may even establish a niche in the hospital and start to feel more at home."

I realized that people were considering me a permanent resident of this place. I never did.

. . .

"I don't know if anyone has told you about the history of your strokes," Dr. Crawford said at another early therapy session. "If no one has, I'd like to let you know what happened."

I raised my eyes, gratefully. Though I'd remembered what had occurred before I'd passed out on the stairs, and I'd been told some of the details surrounding what had transpired at Mount Sinai, I was still unclear about the strokes themselves. I didn't know how strokes affect the body, or why they occur. Most of all, I wanted to know if I would ever speak again.

"There are two basic categories of strokes," Dr. Crawford said. "The first is when someone has a stroke and can't communicate. That's called aphasia. Because it causes damage to the language center of the brain, this variety of stroke is considered a language disorder. People suffering from aphasia can't understand what others say, nor can they speak. This is not the case with you, right?"

I raised my eyes in agreement.

"The second variety of stroke," Dr. Crawford continued, looking down at a piece of paper, "is called anarthria or severe dysarthria. People like you who suffer this type of stroke have sustained neurological damage. Unlike those with aphasia, these folks don't appear to experience difficulty in processing language. While they can think clearly and comprehend what others say, people with anarthria can't speak at all."

I looked at him, grateful that he didn't mince his words.

"Most stroke patients are hemiplegic—that is, the

stroke affects only one side of the body. But you're quadriplegic, meaning the strokes damaged both sides, right?"

I raised my eyes, and a wave of pain washed over me.
But this time, instead of thinking that I'd drown, I felt a
tinge of relief. Knowing the truth gave me a tiny increment
of power over my circumstances.

"You must have had two strokes," Dr. Crawford continued. "The first one—the one you had at home—
affected the left side of your body. The other stroke—
which you experienced at Mount Sinai—had to have affected the right side. Because you were unable to speak and
you were paralyzed on both sides, people thought you were
organic. Yet you could comprehend everything that was
going on around you; that was the tragedy on top of a
tragedy."

I started to cry and raise my eyes at the same time.

"We can speak about specifics as much as you like. I'll
tell you what I know about strokes. Related to the damage,
of course, is the emotional distress that follows. My guess
is that you have a lot of feelings that lie buried inside you
—anger, doubt, frustration, and the like. I'm wondering if
we can find a way for you to express these things."

I looked at him but didn't raise my eyes. I had so many
horrible thoughts about hurting the people who had
harmed me that I didn't know where to begin. I still had
vast mood swings. One moment I'd be so depressed that I'd
give anything to die. The next minute, I'd be so angry that
I'd vow to let nothing kill me. Even though writing had

given me a way to address the emotional questions surrounding my disability, I still reasoned that it might be best to leave these feelings unsaid.

"Though it might be difficult to talk about these things," Dr. Crawford pursued, "I'd at least like to bring up the subject. People with disabilities generally fall into one of a few predominant patterns. Some go into a state of denial and repress their feelings. Others react by being hostile to the world around them. Still others retreat into silence, avoiding human contact altogether. This can result in chronic depression."

I knew that what he said was true—I did have a lot of anger, resentment, and self-pity. My life had been shattered at a time of happiness, and those whom I loved had left me. My anger was so strong that I thought I would burst.

"Sometimes the most direct avenue into these feelings is to talk about your dreams. We could start by exploring any dream you can recall, using the alphabet card Arlene's given us. She's also indicated that it may be possible for you to obtain your own communication device."

He paused. As I thought how impossible this all sounded, Dr. Crawford smiled. "The optimal situation," he said, still smiling, "would be for you to have a portable writing device that could be mounted on your chair. This would enhance our work together. You could write about your dreams, and we could discuss your writing in therapy."

Though I was skeptical, I realized that Dr. Crawford

was willing to speak with me and allow me to express my-self as best I could. I began to trust him. At least he was willing to use the alphabet card to communicate with me. He also had the patience to let me ask questions.

Even though I didn't know what dreams had to do with anything, I was willing to give it a go. I raised my eyes and smiled at Dr. Crawford.

. . .

One afternoon when I was in the solarium working on my poems, I saw a good-looking man standing in the doorway. He was over six feet tall, dressed in a jacket and tie, and looked to be in his early thirties. Beneath a head of short brown hair, his face was clean-cut. He walked over to me.

"Hello," he said. "My name is Bill Ryan. Arlene's as-signed me to be your new volunteer." When he spoke, his brown eyes sparkled.

Though he seemed nervous, he smiled at me and asked if he could stay for a moment, to talk. I raised my eyes, and he seemed to understand what that meant. He walked to where I was sitting in front of the Macintosh and stood be-side my wheelchair.

"Do you mind if I watch?" he asked, looking at the computer. I faced the machine and waited for the light to come to the letter I wanted. I pressed the switch and saw the letter printed. Then the machine started again, at the letter *A*.

Bill didn't interrupt what I was writing. He continued to watch how I used the machine. After a moment, I stopped. I looked at him standing beside me and wondered how I could tell him to take the vacant chair by the wall. I started to write this, but then I had a better idea. I looked at him, then out toward the hallway. I thought it might be best for Bill if we went into the main hall.

Right away, he understood what I was asking. He looked at me, then glanced out to where I was motioning with my eyes. "Like to leave, Julia?" he asked, politely.

I raised my eyes.

He wheeled me out into the sun-filled corridor, and we found a chair near a window. I looked at the chair, and Bill sat down.

He started to talk, first telling me about his job as a tax and investment consultant. He said that he loved kids and that he and his wife wanted to raise a family. He took out a picture of his wife, and I saw a pretty blonde woman with a nice smile and an intelligent face. I wondered why a man with so much going for him would want to volunteer at Goldwater.

"Arlene said you might want some company once in a while."

I looked at his handsome face and thought, if this is the kind of company she'll get me, I'll be glad to entertain seven days a week! To be polite, however, I just raised my eyes.

"She also said you might need some help, that you're

in the process of getting a wheelchair you can operate yourself."

Though I couldn't count on anything for sure, I raised my eyes.

"I thought you might want some help—you know, doing things you can't do by yourself. Maybe you'll need someone to pitch in when you get your wheelchair."

Bill and I became close friends. Even though the tax business is a demanding line of work, he started to visit me often. Because of a recent illness, I'd been moved back to the D ward. The people who lived there had less peer contact than those who resided on other wards. We were also at the bottom of the list to receive rehabilitation therapies. I had therefore decided to live on another ward. I wanted to eat better food, have interactions with other people, and manage the parts of my life that I could, such as scheduling time in speech and OT. The primary hindrance was that I was stuck on the D ward, where my few freedoms were curtailed.

Bill helped me change this. His selfless concern for others amazed me. Even though he barely knew me, he wrote letters on my behalf, asking why, if I wasn't a medical patient, I was being treated like one. He lobbied for my own motorized wheelchair. When the nurses positioned me incorrectly in my manual wheelchair, Bill was sometimes on hand to make me more comfortable. He'd lift me from behind, holding me around the shoulders, and pull me toward him. I felt his chest muscles against my back. His biceps would become taut as he lowered me down gently, back in the chair. Immediately, I felt a relief that seemed immeasurable. Not only that, but the physical contact with a man for the first time in nine years was a great comfort. In Bill's arms, I felt protected and cared for. Though I thanked him many times, he'd shrug it off as if he'd done nothing in particular.

One day, to my delight, my mother and Joan brought in some of my old clothes. But since I had an altogether different body than the one I'd arrived with, they no longer fit. A nurse's aide named Ms. Harvey helped get me some clothes from the basement, but they weren't my style. I wanted something with life in it! I remembered Marilyn Monroe dancing across the stage in that ravishing red gown and crooning "Diamonds Are a Girl's Best Friend." I thought if I couldn't have men in black tuxedos crowding around me, proffering jewels in their open palms, I'd have some pretty clothes. I wanted colors and wild patterns. And yes, I even wanted something sexy once in a while.

I spelled this out to Bill. On his next visit, he brought a mail-order catalogue—a thrilling sight. Here was this good-looking man, eight years my junior, holding up the glossy pages of a women's catalogue, flipping through so I could choose some colorfully feminine clothes. When he got to the brassieres and panties, he blushed. I laughed to see this big man turning red until his ears blazed. Nonetheless, we got past the bras, and I picked out the clothes I wanted. Bill sent the order in.

When the clothes arrived, I had an orange summer dress, green socks, a mauve beret, a silver sequined top, and a black blouse to add to my wardrobe. Purple had always been my favorite color, any shade, any fabric. That day, I think I bought enough of it to last a lifetime. Along with lime greens and yellows, I now had purple pants, a purple belt, and a green and yellow shawl.

I wanted to start dressing right. If I couldn't control what people said about me, if I couldn't speak back or leave the room when a nurse's aide ridiculed me, if I couldn't choose my food or where I lived or when I got up, I'd control the one thing I could: how I dressed. I printed messages to let the nurses know that I wanted to select my clothes every day. This caused a commotion because the nurses and aides complained about how long it took to dress me. They finally figured out that all they had to do was hold up the clothes, item by item. When I spotted what I wanted to wear, I raised my eyes.

I remember my first choice of an outfit: a black blouse with lavender pants, a lavender scarf, black socks, and lavender slippers. I even managed to get the aide to comb my hair and tie it back with a black chiffon ribbon. She kept saying under her breath, "Why do you want to look good? Nobody's looking at you anyway." To her, I guess I was a pain. But I didn't see anything wrong with wanting to feel good about myself. For so long, I'd been stripped of any identity besides that of a sexless piece of meat who had to be turned over or doused with water or funneled full of liquid food that I had begun to think of myself as less than an animal. Part of my personal rehabilitation involved learning how to take care of the parts of my life that I could. Choosing my own clothes was the first step.

For a while, life was as good as I thought it would ever get. I now had four people who cared for me. Not only that, but Joan started visiting me periodically. Sometimes she brought a gift, like the statue of Saint Jude that she placed on a table near my bed. If I couldn't have Judy, I thought, I'd at least have the saint I'd named her for.

One day, the scan control system arrived from California. A mechanic named Mike Acevedo was able to connect it to a motorized wheelchair. But because this was a new system, there were many things that went wrong. When something malfunctioned, the scanner had to be sent to the West Coast for repairs. My scanning system was constantly running out of power, and the internal batteries would last only a few hours at a time. Mike figured out a way to fix the problem. If it weren't for his expertise, I would still be lying in bed.

Whereas Mike got the chair in working order, Bill helped me learn to operate it. He'd charge the battery and talk me through the frustration of adapting to the new chin switch. This was a device that a man named Arnoldo Rios customized for my chair.

Arnoldo was a quadriplegic himself. Someone had struck him over the head with a board, and he'd sustained permanent damage to the fifth cervical bone in his spine.

Despite the severity of his injury, Arnoldo was able to have reconstructive surgery. Part of a bone in his hip had been fused with his spine. He was in traction for so long, he thought he'd never get up again. He told me that it was the sheer power of his will that had allowed him to survive.

Arnoldo did his own therapy. By the time he could walk again, he had learned how to create tools for the disabled. He regained the use of his hands and continued walking for three years before he had to start using a wheelchair. I felt encouraged to see a disabled person accomplishing things for himself. When there was an opening in the OT department, he was hired. He and Joyce collaborated on many patients' equipment, including mine.

Arnoldo made a special table for my wheelchair and an arm that extended up to where my chin would rest when I sat in the chair. At the end of the arm, he positioned a mouth switch. He extended a curved metal pole over the front of my wheelchair, which is where he secured the new scanning device. When I sat in the chair, I faced the dial pointing in the four directions Joyce had described. When the system lit up the direction I wanted to go, I leaned down on the chin switch Arnoldo had positioned for me, and off I'd go.

That was the theory, anyway. Practically speaking, it was months before I could sit in the chair without feeling pain. Then it took more time before I could coordinate my head movements with the lights flashing in front of me. Even though I had people helping me, I became extremely frustrated. More than once, I wanted to give up and throw the whole thing in the river below my window.

Bill stood by me through thick and thin. It took many months before I learned how to operate these machines and was rolling up and down the halls. Yet it was worth all the effort. I could stop when I wanted and go when the feeling struck me. I could finally turn on my own accord and move away from someone who was bothering me. I could go to the far reaches of the hospital building and look out at the river running beyond the fence.

Modern technology gave me more freedom than I'd dreamed possible. Before the strokes, I had taken technology for granted. Cars, radios, the dishwasher—all seemed an ordinary part of reality. I didn't give a second thought to the things that made life convenient. But now, after years of languishing inside the parameters of my five-foot, five-inch body, I thanked every little wire and flashing light, every screw and metal plate and switch that made it possible for me to attain the degree of independence I now had. I felt fortunate to have the technical devices I was using, including the Macintosh, and to have people on hand who knew how to operate and repair them.

I had a letter board that Bill, Dr. Crawford, Arlene, and Joyce used regularly. I used the Macintosh to write my poems and send letters to my family. I also wrote notes to the nurses taking care of me, suggesting ways for them to improve my positioning, asking for certain food, and requesting that I get out of bed earlier in the morning.

Thanks to Joyce, Mike, and Arnoldo, I could now go outside and see where I'd been living for thirteen years.

One day in early spring, Bill asked if he could take me for
a walk. I maneuvered down the hall and out into the hospital's lobby. Bill helped me descend the steep slope of the
driveway. Then I drove around the edge of the green lawn.
Swallows twittered in the high branches of the sycamore
trees, and I could make out new leaf shoots on the lower
limbs.

Along the waterfront, a row of cherry trees was in full
bloom. The blossoms were just beginning to fall. Bill
pushed me down to the embankment and said this was the
East River. Beyond it, on Franklin D. Roosevelt Drive,
the cars rushed past. To the south, just on the other side of
the river, was the shimmering tower of the United Nations.
Near it, among the clusters of high-rise apartments, loomed
the decorative spirals of the Chrysler Building. Nestled farther back in the city's maze of streets was the sharp point
of the Empire State Building. To the north was a structure
Bill called the Queensboro Bridge, which I must have
crossed when I was taken back and forth from Bellevue. On
the other side of this bridge, I could make out the boxed
shapes of tram cars lifting over the river, carrying people
across to Manhattan. I remembered a nurse once saying that
about two miles to the north of the tram was Gracie Man-
sion, the home of New York City's mayor. As Bill wheeled
me up the on-ramp and into a car, I wondered if the mayor
had ever visited Goldwater Hospital.

Inside the tram, Bill rolled me close to a window. The car eased up on its thick steel cords, and we were soon rising into the air. Across the water, I could see Manhattan's wealthy Upper East Side. I remembered, as a girl, hearing people speak in awe of those who lived in this section of the city. It was as if they were a special breed of humanity, an elite class of people who wore expensive furs, ate caviar, and drank the finest French wines. It gave me a pang of sorrow to realize that the hospital and those luxurious apartments were separated by a body of water just a quarter-mile wide.

The tram stopped at Sixtieth Street and Second Avenue. Bill led me down another ramp and onto the crowded Saturday street. The noise overwhelmed me, as did the cars, the bustle, and the women with their leather handbags and stylish sunglasses. A short girl with red hair passed by, pushing a baby carriage containing twins. Even though it was a weekend, I saw men dressed in suits and carrying briefcases.

We crossed to Fifty-ninth Street.

"I thought we might go to Bloomingdale's," Bill offered.

When he saw how my eyes lit up, he pushed my chair in the direction of Third Avenue. Up and down the street, people spilled out of clothing stores and antique shops. We passed a tee-shirt shop, and I saw a display in the window that shocked me. It was a white shirt with a tombstone printed on it that read Elvis Presley, 1935–1977. Beneath the tombstone were the words Visit Elvis at Graceland.

Long May He Live. Bill saw me staring at the window and stopped my wheelchair in front of it. I saw more detail on the shirt, including sprays of red roses wreathed around his youthful portrait. He appeared as he had when I'd first seen him in 1956, smiling and devastatingly handsome.

"You know he died, right?" Bill asked.

I stared straight at him, partly in disbelief and partly to answer his question.

"Yes, the King died last year, 1977. There were all these rumors about his horrible personal life and his drug use. I used to listen to his music, so it really disturbed me when they found him dead. A heart attack or something. He's buried in Memphis, and I hear his gravesite has become a huge tourist attraction."

Bill's voice trailed off and I remembered those first days of my marriage to Jim. Elvis, I recalled, was just beginning to become famous and I had seen his picture in a magazine. He was sitting on a motorcycle, and I'd thought there could be no man more handsome on this earth. And now he was dead. I felt like a part of my young adulthood was dead, too, and I wondered what other events had transpired in the world during the years that I lay immobile in the hospital.

Bill turned my wheelchair away from the window, and I saw an Episcopal church gracing the middle of the block, its sturdy pillars as guarded and implacable as the silence I'd been living in. As we passed the church I said a prayer for Elvis.

We crossed Third Avenue, and I saw Bloomingdale's. Throngs of people bustled in and out the glass doors. As we approached the entrance, the noise of so many clamoring voices frightened me.

Inside, it was quieter. I thought it would be easier to relax. But I wasn't ready for the stares. We weren't there five seconds before people started gawking. While it might have been unusual for a lady to be pushed in a wheelchair down the aisles of New York's finest department store, I thought people would have had better manners.

Suddenly, I realized how similarly people had reacted to me back when they had raved about my beauty. I remembered the time when I was twenty-two, driving home from work one summer afternoon. I was in my blue convertible, listening to pop songs on the radio as I went home to the Beach Thirty-third Street apartment I shared with Joan. A new song called "Rock Around the Clock" came on and I tapped my hand against the steering wheel to its infectious beat. I was stopped at a red light when, out of nowhere, a guy in a silver Plymouth started honking his horn. He yelled out his window, "Hey, gorgeous. How about a ride down to the beach?" I turned up my radio and tried to ignore him. The light changed to green, and I pressed the accelerator hard. He thought I was playing a game. He followed me, honking his horn and tailgating. I realized that this idiot would probably follow me to my very doorstep. I decided to pull off at the 101st police precinct on Mott Avenue. I got out of my car and stepped up the stairs and into the station. I turned and saw the guy in the silver coupe high-tailing it in the opposite direction.

Now, in Bloomingdale's, instead of people gawking because they found me sexy, they stared because they found me ugly. But I was so happy to be outside of the hospital that I didn't care. I was too busy reveling in a world of opulence, pungent perfumes, and brightly patterned clothes. I watched people smile at each other. A blonde woman was giving away samples of perfume. As we went by, she looked at me. She asked Bill if she could give me a whiff. She sprayed some on the back of my neck, and I only wished that I'd been able to walk. I would have tried on light dresses and tank tops, flowery blouses and earrings.

The best thing about Bloomingdale's was the men. There were men in suits and men in jeans, men with mustaches and clean-shaven men who smelled of musky cologne. This was the first time in nine years that I had smelled the robust, lingering scent of men. They wore their hair longer than I'd remembered, and they dressed in brighter colors. Some men wore wildly colorful ties. One man walked by in tight white pants. This reminded me of two guys, Joe and Ed, who used to meet Joanie and me for drinks at the Runway Inn. Their white pants were always so tight that I couldn't take my eyes away. And now, in Bloomingdale's, this man was so handsome that even after he gave me a perplexed look of disgust, I forgave him because of those pants.

Bill touched a silk scarf to my shoulders. It was as soft as a baby's skin. I saw a wall of brassieres and smiled, remembering how Bill had blushed the day we looked through the catalogue. Camel-hair coats and watches and bikinis, men's underwear and what Bill called bell-bottom jeans—you name it, this place had it.

By the time we left the store, I was exhausted. As Bill pushed me back to the Sixtieth Street tram station, dusk was falling around us. He got me into a car, and we rose, once more, out over the river. The sunset glowed deep orange and scarlet. Beneath us, the water sparkled like a strand of green jewels. I felt Bill's hands on my shoulders, and I looked at the people seated around me. Though some of them were looking at me, most were staring out the window at the lovely colors reflected off the water and into the clouds above. Everything looked hazy and romantic. I turned toward Bill. I imagined that I was on a date with him, my first in sixteen years.

As we neared the island, I could see a cluster of buildings. This was the hospital. Made of gray and tan bricks, it had five wings and looked to be four or five stories high.

"Someone told me that this place used to be called Welfare Island," Bill explained. "They used to have different hospitals for various diseases, including a smallpox hospital. There even used to be a lunatic asylum here."

Still is, I thought, as we dipped down into the tram station. The doors opened, and as Bill wheeled me out, I saw a sign: Franklin D. Roosevelt Goldwater Memorial Hospital. I wanted to tell Bill how grateful I was to him. He had given me a day of happiness, my first in thirteen years. All along the walk back, as Bill pushed me, I wept. Now, I'd have to go back in.

Chapter Twelve

HAYFIELD IN
THE OCEAN

I dreamed there was a hayfield
In the ocean
Looked at the full moon
Asked myself
Why oh why
Am I in a tunnel
Why oh why oh why
Do I see this imaginary
Tunnel! Has dark morbid clouds
With hands sprawling and crawling
Into the golden wheat field. I ventured
Out: the cool waters! of green
Ocean. Seagulls flew above my regret
Wheat field, my ocean so hard to forget.

After my trip to Bloomingdale's, my sense of time changed dramatically. Ever since the strokes, it had been difficult for me to differentiate between hours, days, and weeks. My rooms had contained no calendars or clocks. Seeing Joyce's watch the day she fed me Jell-O had been my first chance in all the years of hospital life to know the time. But now I found myself able to keep track of what was going on around me in a cohesion of days and months.

Throughout the 1980s I experienced a flurry of activity that kept me in a constant state of change. It began with the departure of both Arlene and Joyce within a year and a half of each other. Just as I was becoming determined to have an audible voice in the world, I now had to contend with the loss of my two greatest allies.

When Arlene told me in 1980 that she was taking a better job, I panicked. Who would deliver my messages to the ward? Who would speak on my behalf and intervene when I wanted to communicate with the nurses? Who would schedule time for me to use the computer, and who would stand up for my rights?

During our last speech therapy session together, as light from the window shone down on Arlene's face and her light-blue blouse, she held the alphabet card. I W-I-L-L M-I-S-S Y-O-U A-N-D T-H-I-N-K O-F Y-O-U O-F-T-E-N, I spelled.

"I'll miss you, too, Julia," Arlene responded. "We've done important work together."

D-O-N-T K-N-O-W H-O-W I-L-L G-E-T B-Y W-I-T-H-O-U-T Y-O-U.

"Think of it this way: When you have to take new hurdles alone, remind yourself that I *know* you can do it.

With or without me, you must continue fighting. That's what any life is about, right?"

I was really crying then, and the letters on the alphabet card became blurry. "Focus on what you have and what you're able to do, Julia," Arlene suggested. "Set goals for yourself and devise ways to complete them. My leaving may be one way for you to take control of your own life."

I looked up at Arlene and heard a new voice in my head: I will challenge myself! What others can't do for me, I'll struggle to accomplish on my own. On the way back to my room, I thought about my goals. I wanted to move to the A ward and write as much as possible. I also wanted to participate in ensuring the quality of my care, making as many of my own decisions as I could. Most important of all, I determined to obtain my own writing device.

During my last occupational therapy session with Joyce in March 1981, she touched my shoulder and said, "You might want to view my leaving as a door opening for you, Julia. Though it may be scary to go through that door, I think you'll find a higher degree of independence if you take the chance and wheel across. My leaving might give you a clear indication of what you can do for yourself."

I took her advice to heart, and on a spring night not long afterward, as a nurse was lifting me in the Hoyer and putting me to bed, I felt a core of strength take hold inside me. As rain struck the window near my bed, I thought of my list of goals. No matter how long it took or how much I'd have to struggle, I vowed to let nothing defeat me.

The first thing that threatened to stop me was a bad case of pneumonia, which forced me to stay in bed. The days stretched into weeks, and the temperate New York spring turned into the long, humid summer. Because of having to lie still for so long, I lost some of the flexibility in my hip joints. As a result, when I was well enough to be positioned in my wheelchair, I could sit up for only an hour or two at a time. I resumed twice-weekly occupational therapy sessions.

One day when I was daydreaming about owning my own writing device, I received a welcome surprise: a visit from my father. Dressed in a red and black checkered shirt, pants, suspenders, his old hunting cap, and his brown hunting boots, he walked over to me, leaned down over my bed, and kissed me on the cheek. I could smell cigarette smoke mingled with the odor of whiskey on his breath. His face appeared swollen, and I noticed that he'd lost a lot of weight. "Hiya, Julie," he said. "I wanted to see you on my way to go deer hunting."

His voice sounded rough and gravelly, not as deep and resonant as it used to. Though he still talked like a man drunk on an overflowing cup of life, my father appeared to have lost his youthful zeal. He gave me a wink and started to laugh. The sound of his laughter made me feel good. I laughed, too, when I realized that he meant D-E-A-R hunting: he had a new girlfriend.

"I just wanted to check on you, and to bring you a present," my father said. He went out of the room and returned with a television set. "Thought you might like to see the tube every once in a while. I know how you used to like *I Love Lucy* and *Mission Impossible*. Don't really watch TV myself, but I thought you might find something to keep you occupied." He set the TV on the table across from my bed. Though I didn't know if the nurses would cooperate and let me watch it, I was happy all the same. Dad plugged it in and turned it on. To my delighted surprise, there was a beautiful blonde woman in a blue strapless dress giving a walking tour of Paris. She passed a restaurant she said was one of the most renowned in the city, the Café Flore, and told how it had once been a meeting place for famous writers. I took this as an omen for my successful future as a poet and reveled in the fact that I now had a link to the outside world.

"Remember the times we'd go upstate, Julie?" my father asked as he turned down the volume on the TV. "Those were the good ol' days. A rifle in my hand, a deer over the next rise, and the smell of the wet earth all around us. Remember it, honey?" The memory filled me with both pleasure and sorrow. In my mind I was fourteen again, getting out of bed and going downstairs to make coffee before my father and I went hunting.

He stayed only a short while, talking about how beautiful the countryside would be in the fall. He didn't mention my mother or anyone else in my family. He didn't comment about the hospital or use the alphabet card near my bed. I think he came just to give me the TV and to show me that he knew I was aware. He also wanted to share his secret with me, as he had done when I was young. Despite my sadness at not having seen him in a few years, I was glad that he still considered me part of his forbidden world. Before leaving, he touched my forehead and turned up the volume on the TV. He said he'd be back to see me, but I had a feeling he wouldn't visit again.

Slowly the joints in my hips continued to heal. On days when I was bedridden, I watched TV. I saw some things that shocked me, including a newsclip of a band that played the worst music I'd ever heard—nothing like Elvis. The audience seemed crazed, as if high on drugs. They were all wearing leather and had earrings in their noses, and the crowd moved in a frenzy across the screen. One teenager jumped on stage and threw up. The scene was utterly shocking. Before long the image changed to a war zone in El Salvador, a country I'd never even heard of. The commentator referred to U.S. military intervention in a place called Honduras, and I remembered back in 1969 hearing the nurses talk about war. I thought it couldn't possibly be the same war as the one they were crying over back then. The screen showed a dark street and some women in black standing near what appeared to be dead bodies.

The image shifted again, and I saw a vaguely familiar man wearing an expensive-looking suit. An American flag was draped behind him, and a caption appeared at the bottom of the screen. I could make out the words "Ronald Reagan—Fortieth President of the United States." John F.

Kennedy had been the thirty-fifth president, and Lyndon Johnson had followed in his footsteps after the assassination in 1963. But who had followed him? Reagan talked about defending the United States against infiltration from abroad, especially from the Russians. He also said something about domestic spending cuts and the importance of nuclear weapons. I remembered the bomb that had been dropped on the Japanese in 1945 and the shelter that my father had made my family hide in. Back then, when we listened to the news on the radio, Dad had cheered and said nasty things about "the Communists." After all my time in seclusion, it seemed that the problems of the world were the same, only different people were talking about them.

Though I was fascinated to see how much the world had changed since I'd been in the hospital, I was relieved when I could return to my wheelchair and do other things besides watch TV. As the fall of 1981 turned to winter, I'd roll into the halls, park at a window somewhere, and look out at naked branches of the trees below, the river running past, and cars moving in the distance. I sat looking at all that activity, longing for the day when I could write about it at my leisure. I felt my will strong inside me. *Why not will a writing device into my life?* I thought, imagining a classy one right beside the wheelchair switch on the table before me. I kept saying to myself, *I want a writing device. I refuse to live in silence.*

The months passed and I attended OT sessions and visits for psychotherapy with Dr. Crawford. I used the machine in the speech therapy department to print repeated requests for my own writing device. Someone in speech told me that Medicaid was slow and that it might take years until I heard back from the agency, which might even deny me such a device.

One morning in October 1982, I was visited by a doctor and a nurse in my room on the D ward. "Good afternoon, Mrs. Tavalaro," the doctor said. This was the first time I remembered any doctor calling me by my name. He had a kind smile and looked me in the eye when he spoke. "We've been authorized to remove the cannula tube for a trial period of a few months."

I looked at him in disbelief. The tube that had been placed in my throat to help me breathe and to prevent me from choking on my own saliva had been in for so long that it felt like an appendage. I hardly noticed it anymore and wondered what it would be like to live without it. As the nurse held a light, I felt the doctor jiggle the tube, then slip it from my throat. I was scared and excited at the same time. For a moment, neither the doctor nor the nurse spoke. The doctor gave me a questioning look, but I was afraid to attempt speech. I stayed still, moving neither my neck nor my eyes. I told myself that if I could speak, I'd ask someone to call Arlene and Joyce so I could thank them for all their support and expertise.

"How's that, Mrs. Tavalaro?" the doctor finally asked. I imagined the voice in my head saying, "It's fine, doctor. I can talk now." As I thought this, I tried to say hello. My throat felt tight, like someone's hands were circling it. I tried to move my tongue, but it felt heavy as lead. I tried to open my mouth and say the word, but my jaw wouldn't move. I heard only a groan. Though it was louder than the sounds I could previously make, I couldn't produce the word: no "H" sound, no "E," no "L," no "O." The sound came out as a low, flat moan.

After the doctor left, I realized that I possessed what Arlene had termed "voice," but I wasn't able to speak in words. Though I'd intuitively known all along that I would never speak again, a small part of me had retained that hope for nearly sixteen years. Now I was forced to face the painful truth. Out of nowhere, I heard Arlene's voice of encouragement saying, "You have such beautiful eyes. They're the parts of your body you control best. Use them to point to things." I remembered how I'd "spoken" to Bill with my eyes that first time he'd seen me working on the computer. I looked around the room, saw the woman sleeping in the bed next to mine, and heard the sound of a machine breathing for her. At least I could breathe for myself, I thought.

For the first time since I'd been in the hospital, I consciously sought to reassure myself. I started thinking that perhaps my inability to speak made me a unique person. I could now make sounds I'd been unable to make before. These sounds gave me a tool, however rudimentary, with which to direct my life. I could make soft sounds to get someone's attention or howl loudly to indicate "no." I had various tones that punctuated my deep, low note of rage. Grunts, groans, humming vibrations—these, coupled with eye movements, would be my language.

I began emitting sounds to get people's attention. If I needed someone to wipe my mouth with a tissue, I'd groan at a nurse in the room. When she looked at me, I'd glance at the box of tissues, then at the nurse, then back at the tissues. If my legs hurt, causing a pain sharp as bolts of electricity to shoot up my thighs, hips, and back, I'd look at my legs and cry as loudly as I could. Sometimes a nurse would notice these sounds and eye motions, and she'd adjust my legs closer together or grab a tissue and wipe my mouth. Immediately, I'd beam my eyes at her in gratitude.

Once more, I started attending speech therapy activities, this time to increase the volume and vary the sounds of the vocalizations I could now emit. I figured that I would use my new vocalizations to their full capacity and not allow others to do things to me without my consent. But I soon found out the consequences of using these sounds when an aide came to feed me less than a month after the tube was removed.

It was a cold day in early November, and the aide seemed impatient. I was hungry, and she was taking her time. She came into the room, fiddled with the television my father had brought me, watched it for a minute, then left. My food was sitting on the table for more than half an hour. Finally, the aide returned. I wanted to get her attention, so I hummed softly. She didn't notice, so I groaned.

Still, she ignored me. I groaned louder, then started to cry. She turned up the volume on my TV, and I howled. I was leaning back in my chair as far as I could, arching my back and crying in an attempt to get her to feed me. She said, "You better stop your crying or I'm not doing nothing for you, Tavalaro." When I didn't stop crying, she rushed over to the sink, took a washcloth, and stuffed it into my mouth.

I couldn't breathe. The aide stood over me, her hands on her hips. After what I've lived through, I thought, I'm not going to die at the hands of some idiot who would rather watch the news than do her job. "Had enough, bitch?" she demanded. "You done playing with me?" I was at her mercy. She went over to the TV, switched stations, then walked nonchalantly to where I was sitting. She reached over and slid the cloth out of my mouth. Quickly, before I had time to catch my breath, she started stuffing yogurt into my mouth. Only when I began to choke did she stop long enough for me to breathe.

After she finished feeding me, I remembered the pledge I'd made to take care of myself. I had a wheelchair and a mouth switch with which to operate it. I had an alphabet card, and I knew the layout of the hospital, especially where the office of the director of nursing was. I decided to go there and make a formal complaint.

I parked my wheelchair in front of the office and refused to move until someone came out to speak with me. Finally, the director of nursing emerged, and I spelled out what had happened. Within a month the woman who had stuffed the cloth into my mouth was no longer working on the D ward.

Right after this incident, I was transferred to the C ward. I saw this as an indication that the hospital was preparing for my move to the A ward. But that wasn't the case; I had to remain on the C ward for three more years. This was a period of relative calm. I tried to write poetry in the speech therapy office and continued to hope for an augmentative device and a bed on the A ward.

Then one night in late December 1984, I had a dream in which my paternal grandmother, Nana, appeared on a snow-covered hill that I didn't recognize. Pine trees were frozen solid all around her, and I saw her face reflected in fragments of ice. The wind blew in flurries, raising the powdered snow into shapes that resembled bodies. There were no people or houses in sight. I remembered when Nana had come to me the day I had almost died in Bellevue more than ten years earlier and the time she appeared just before Arlene introduced herself. Once again, she held out her hand and summoned me to come into her warm embrace. The wind whipped around her, but it didn't ruffle her hair or wrinkle the black dress she was wearing. Unlike before, no matter how long she stood in the cold, I didn't want to approach her. I looked at her with love, but I no longer needed her comfort.

A few days after I had this dream, Joan and Dr. Crawford came into my room. I was shocked to see my sister, since she had been absent for more than two years. Joanie was crying, and Dr. Crawford looked solemn. For a moment, neither of them spoke. Then Joanie said, "Julie, I've come with some bad news." She wiped her eyes with a tissue, and I knew something terrible had happened. "Dad died two nights ago, the twenty-eighth of December. It was cancer." This was the first time I'd heard about my father's illness. Joanie put her arms around me, and I cried quietly, feeling like I had lost a part of myself.

. . .

All through the mid-1980s while I waited to be moved to the A ward, I watched TV, attended therapy sessions with Dr. Crawford, and went to speech therapy and OT activities. To be near books, I started going more often to the library. I continued listening to recordings of books on tape, mostly romances. As a young woman, I had devoured romance novels, but now they struck me as tawdry and false. I no longer believed in them.

When I had almost given up on ever obtaining a writing device and moving to the A ward, Bill wrote a letter to the hospital's executive director. In no uncertain terms, he implied that the hospital was stalling my requests. A couple of weeks later, a nurse came to tell me some good news: my request to relocate to the A ward had finally been approved! I just had to wait until a bed became available.

I thought I'd have to be patient for a few weeks or months at most. I went about my business, thinking that any day some administrator would inform me that a bed was vacant. But the weeks spun into months, and still nothing transpired. The months turned into years. It wasn't until 1986—nearly six years after I'd made my first request—that I was finally transferred. The day of the move, I was happy and scared at the same time. I didn't know what to expect or whether I would fit in. But I didn't have much time to worry, for I soon met a nurse's aide, Deloris Cook, who helped make my transition to the A ward a smooth one.

Kindhearted and cheerful, Deloris had a big laugh. "I'm Cook," she said, "that's what everybody calls me." She smiled then, and I had the feeling that I could trust her. Pretty soon we were on a first-name basis. I watched her routine as she moved through the ward with great energy, smiling and laughing frequently, calling the Goldwater residents by their names, and joking whenever possible. This was a woman with a big spirit, I thought. I want to become her friend.

Soon, Deloris started saying hello to me whenever she arrived for her evening shift. If I was in a foul mood, she'd call me "skinny little thing" and tell me how beautiful my skin was. If I was sad, she'd crack a joke. She'd often take the time to let me spell messages on the alphabet card. Right away, she seemed to understand that I wanted the nurses to take my opinion into consideration when caring for me. Deloris made me feel like I was her equal. She'd buy olive oil and give me daily rubdowns to keep my skin supple. While gently massaging the oil into my skin, she'd say, "Gonna make you good and slick, darlin', so you can slide down easy in your chair." She'd even kid about herself. "Julia," she'd say, "do you think I'm losing weight? I want to get me a boyfriend." I'd tease her by spelling N-O on the alphabet card. Or I'd give her a dab of perfume that Bill had bought me. "What am I supposed to do," she'd ask, "wear this on a date?" I'd raise my eyes. "And that's supposed to get me a man, huh?" I'd smile, thinking how my mother used to say that perfume was for *putta*.

One day I received an official summons for jury duty. Deloris read it with a straight face, and I immediately started to worry—how would I communicate in court? Then Deloris started to laugh. "Now we know who the really crazy people are," she said. "Let's give them a run for their money. What do you say?"

I raised my eyes enthusiastically. A-S-K F-O-R S-P-E-C-I-A-L E-S-C-O-R-T, I spelled.

"Okay," Deloris said. "'Please send us money for a cab. Better yet, send an ambulance. If you can't do that, would you kindly send the mayor of New York—we need an escort.' How's that?" she asked, looking up from the paper.

We both started to laugh. At first I was laughing at Deloris's lack of concern for the possible ramifications of what we were doing. Then I started laughing at the ridiculousness of being stranded in this wheelchair, at the absurdity of losing my family because my condition frightened them, at being transformed from a raving beauty who couldn't keep men away to a woman who, though I remained the same person inside, couldn't get a man to hold me if I tried.

I laughed at mashed food and the smell of urine in the halls, at the people who gawked at me in Bloomingdale's, and at the doctors who, for six years, had not even bothered to find out whether I was aware. I laughed until I cried.

And then I really started to cry—for my lost daughter, my silenced voice, my twisted limbs. I cried for the pain throbbing down my back, and for the times I'd wanted to die. Deloris looked at me, and I saw tears running down her face, too.

"What are we going to do with you, Julia?" she said, wiping her eyes. She touched my shoulder, and I felt grateful that I'd been moved to her ward.

Returning to the jury-duty form, we filled it out in detail, falsifying my birthdate, place of birth, race, and profession. Instead of being fifty-one, I was now twenty-five. Instead of being from Inwood, Long Island, I was now from the Caribbean. Instead of being white, I was now black. Instead of being a disabled person, I was a Las Vegas showgirl.

When Deloris showed the letter to the other aides and nurses, they began to joke with me, calling me a black girl and addressing me with fake accents. For the first time, they seemed to realize that I was not unlike them. Though each day was still difficult, I generally felt more lighthearted and hopeful. Despite a wheelchair accident in 1986 that fractured my left tibia and fibula, leaving me with permanent leg problems, I maintained hope and focused on the future.

Soon I had something that made all the difference in that future: my own augmentative device! In 1987—five years after my first request and ten years after I had first started using the Macintosh and Porta Printer—I now had a device I could call my own. It was a scanning machine similar to the ones I'd used with Arlene. A red light flashed letter by letter across a screen set on the table Arnoldo had made for me. He positioned a second switch to the right of my chair, and when the light flashed at the appropriate letter, I'd press this switch with my right cheek. The letter would be typed on a portable printer set on the left side of my table. Then the scan would return to the letter *A*, and I'd wait until the light blinked on the next letter I'd chosen. Now I could work on my poems in earnest.

I immediately established a routine. The nurses would get me up around noon, I'd have some lunch, and then I'd set to work writing. My goal was to write one poem per day, but I'd sometimes write two or three before stopping at the dinner hour. After dinner I'd be at it again, staring at the red dot's endless cycle from which I made language.

I'd had my writing device for only a few months when someone from the recreational therapy office came to invite me to a writing class that was offered in the hospital. Even before the person from recreational therapy finished telling me about it, I realized that this class was the opportunity

I'd been waiting for. Over and over I raised my eyes as high as I could.

One day in the fall of 1987 when the leaves were changing from green to vibrant reds and yellows, I entered my first writing class, at the age of fifty-two. The workshop had been conceived in 1985 by a poet named Sharon Olds and an organization called Very Special Arts. I discovered that this organization's founder was none other than Jean Kennedy Smith, John F. Kennedy's sister. Sharon was an adjunct professor at New York University (NYU), and she, along with such writers as Erika Duncan, Carolyn Forché, Allen Ginsberg, and Ruth Stone, conducted the classes those first two years.

The day I joined the workshop, I was one of twelve Goldwater residents who formed a circle in the hospital's library. All of us were in wheelchairs, and most of us did not have the use of our hands. Some of us spoke, and others had to use augmentative devices or alphabet boards with pictures across them. Our disabilities spanned a wide range—multiple sclerosis, cerebral palsy, strokes, spinal cord injuries, complications due to drug overdoses—and most of us had lived in Goldwater a number of years. We introduced ourselves and said where we were born, and the discussion that followed centered around how we, as unique individuals from various parts of the world, had common ground.

This workshop and the ones I was to participate in for the next six years were team-taught by three NYU graduate students. Each semester, every Goldwater writer was paired with one of the student-teachers, who would visit us once a week in our rooms. Since I couldn't read my work aloud, this phase of the workshop was particularly important. My tutors, as I came to call these students, would read my poems to me and offer helpful criticism. They'd also talk about the writing process, current events, hospital life, and movies.

For four years I continued to write daily, producing more than two hundred poems. But I felt that some element of risk was lacking in my work. It wasn't until the fall semester of 1991, when Dana Levin, Ernie Munick, and Richard Tayson taught the class, that I was able to let go of my fears and begin writing my best poems.

Richard was my tutor for that semester. He was tall and thin and had a sexy smile. When he'd visit the ward, Deloris would tease me about having a new boyfriend. From the start, Richard took my writing seriously. Though he didn't ask personal questions, he'd inquire about my writing method. When I told him that I often memorized my poems before I wrote them on my augmentative device, he seemed impressed. He watched me write and marveled at my patience. "How do you do it?" he once asked. "You must be an angel from another world to be able to sit and watch that red light flash endlessly through the alphabet!" I looked up at him, then over at the alphabet card. N-O-T A-N A-N-G-E-L. J-U-S-T H-E-L-L-B-E-N-T O-N P-O-E-T-R-Y.

During that semester, Richard encouraged me to write about parts of my life that had been enveloped in silence. "What about your anger," he'd say, "or your feelings for men? What about sadness and fear?" I had no ready answer to these questions.

Not long afterward, Richard brought in a print of Van Gogh's painting *Crows Flying over a Cornfield.* I kept staring at that painting—it seemed so ominous with those black birds flying over the golden wheat. I didn't quite know what to make of it, but something in this painting resonated with the pain in my life. The painter must have experienced an isolation as tightly sealed as my own.

That night, I dreamed I saw myself in a field. Birds hovered over me, and golden wheat brushed my thighs. As I walked through the field, I could hear the flapping of wings and the rustling of wheat stalks in the wind. I heard my baby girl crying and the sound of my parents' voices rising in argument. I could feel water pooling around my feet, and I saw an ocean off in the distance. Then the wheat transformed into the gold carpet I felt beneath my body the night I'd passed out in the house on Roosevelt Street. In the dream, as I looked down at my feet, I felt my spirit fly out of me and float above the earth.

The next day I wrote "Hayfield in the Ocean." Ever since I'd been at Goldwater, I'd craved release from not only my paralyzed body but the institution itself. This poem allowed me to escape in my imagination, momentarily freeing me from pain.

Writing this poem gave me confidence to explore the subjects I'd left unsaid. Though I'd written about Judy, I realized that I'd been avoiding the deep hurt I still felt because of her absence. I had no way to reconcile the fact that in the years between my awakening from the coma and my participation in the writing workshops, I had seen Judy fewer than ten times.

I set to work writing poems that, for the first time, touched on the loss of my daughter. I went back to the night of the strokes, back to the day in the garden when I taught her the names of the flowers. I returned to the time she came to ask for some money to buy a used car. Finally, I wrote about sometimes hearing her voice in my room and about hoping for a reconciliation. With each poem, I furthered my understanding of how my strokes had affected her life.

After I'd been working for some time on these poems, I received a surprise visit from Judy. She came to tell me that she was engaged and that she and her fiancé, Cary, would be married on Valentine's Day, 1992. I thought of my marriage to Jim and found the coincidence of wedding dates painful. But then I thought that it might bring Judy and me closer together. Though I wasn't invited to the wedding, she had come that day to show me her engagement ring. She held out her hand, and I was truly happy for her. Though I didn't see her again for three years, I was grateful that she let me in on the news.

From 1991 through 1993, I continued to work on my

poems and began to think seriously about publishing them. "Anger" was printed in the magazine *Breakthrough*, and this gave me hope that my other poems could be published as well. I started organizing the poems in my mind, placing them side by side in my imagination to see how they would modify and resonate with each other. As I had done with the augmentative device, I consciously set out to will the necessary elements into place that would allow me to publish my work.

In the fall of 1993, Richard was hired to coordinate the NYU/Goldwater writing workshops. When in the hospital, he would stop by to see how I was doing. I-M W-R-I-T-I-N-G A B-O-O-K, I told him one day. W-O-U-L-D Y-O-U H-E-L-P M-E? He said he would. He obtained copies of all the work I'd written to date, and we spent much of October and November reading the poems. We developed a method of judging each poem's effectiveness. Richard would read the poem twice, and each of us would rate it on a scale of one to ten. After reading all the poems, we kept the ones that had garnered a rating of seven or higher. Together, we sorted through these poems, looking for a way to organize them.

Before we'd completed this process, I was invited to participate in a poetry reading at NYU. On October 29, 1993, a number of Goldwater writers were taken in a hospital van to the Randolph Sommerville Theater on Washington Square East in Manhattan's West Village. When I was rolled into the theater, I saw that it was packed, and I could feel an electric excitement in the air. To a crowd of more than two hundred people, Gwendolyn Brooks, Yevgeny Yevtushenko, Sharon Olds, and Cornelius Eady read samples of the Goldwater poets' works. I felt ecstatic when Sharon walked on stage in a black dress and hot-pink high heels. She read my poems in a clear voice that sounded like a small bell chiming.

After we left the reading, the stars looked closer and the moon seemed to embody the miracle of the universe. I smelled the fragrances of late fall and thought how all the writers from Goldwater had done something important that night. I felt more sure than ever that I'd found my calling, and I redoubled my efforts to compile my poems into a book.

One day around Christmas, Richard suggested that I try writing some prose. "Just for fun," he said, "to see what you come up with." Though it turned out to be anything but fun, I started writing about my childhood and what it had been like to grow up in my family. I found the work of writing such long sentences excruciating, but I started thinking that a book of my experiences in prose interspersed with poems would offer a wider understanding of what it was like to live with a disability.

Then came the opportunity I'd been waiting for. In January 1994, I received a visit from Michael Kaufman, a writer at the *New York Times* who wanted to interview me for a story about my life. I was honored and quickly accepted his invitation. His article appeared on January 15, 1994, along with four of my poems and part of a fifth. There was even a picture of me in my wheelchair with my alphabet card lying on the table in front of me. I was overjoyed! Though I no longer looked like Marilyn Monroe, I was proud to be smiling up at everyone who read the paper that day.

Then came the offer of a lifetime: a publisher called Kodansha America wanted to publish my book! Richard told me that Kodansha's vice-president, Minato Asakawa, had read the article in the *New York Times* and had contacted him to help me write the book. It gave me a surge of confidence to know that Kodansha believed in me enough to back my writing. I now had permission to speak about my experience of institutional life.

After nearly two years of work on the book, I got another surprise. One morning in late December 1995, a nurse came in to tell me that Judy was making a visit. When Judy walked into my room, she was holding a baby. I saw my daughter's lithe body, those deep green eyes, her long brown hair, and the narrow Horwat face. *That's my little girl*, I thought, fighting back my anger and tears, trying to forget the fact that she was no longer little—she was thirty.

"This is Harrison," she said, "my new baby." I looked in amazement at the boy. "And this is my husband, Cary." He had a kind face, dark eyes, black hair, and a sturdy build.

"Harrison's one year old now," Judy continued, handing the baby to Cary. "He was born on January 31, 1995. That was your sixtieth birthday, right?"

I raised my eyes. I didn't even know I had a grand-child, let alone one who shared my birthdate. All through Judy's childhood, I had been locked away in this hospital. Now I was about to miss my grandson's youth, too. But then I took it as a sign: I realized that Judy would not easily forget me if she had a son who shared my birthdate.

Judy took up the alphabet card and started moving her finger across the letters. She concentrated hard, and I knew that she was struggling to accept me. Each letter was a mountain we were climbing together for the first time. N-I-C-E S-E-E-I-N-G U A-F-T-E-R S-U-C-H A L-O-N-G T-I-M-E, I spelled. My daughter's eyes filled with tears. She didn't say anything, and I realized how difficult her life must have been without me. I felt my anger melt away, and I began to forgive her.

Y-O-U-R B-A-B-Y I-S G-O-R-G-E-O-U-S. "Yes, Mom, we think so too," she said, wiping her eyes and smil-ing at Cary. "And you haven't even seen him up close, Mrs. Tavalaro," Cary chimed in. "Want me to sit him in front of you in your wheelchair?"

I raised my eyes, and the next thing I knew, I had a beautiful baby boy sitting on the Plexiglas table in front of me, three inches from my face. He had on a white jumper and smelled of baby powder. Judy took the blue knitted cap off his head. Harrison reached his hand up, and I felt his fingers on my face.

"He really likes you," Judy said, glancing toward her husband. "Look at the way he wants to touch you. He doesn't do that with most people. He's kinda shy."

I felt Harrison's fingers on my jaw, my lips, my eyes, and I thought of those days so long ago when I would sit in the backyard with Judy and let her little fingers touch my face. Now, Harrison was exploring my hands, unafraid to touch my marble-colored knuckles and my tightly clenched fists. He looked up at me and made cooing sounds. I wanted to hug and kiss him and tell him how grateful I was to be seeing him.

Judy took a new leather bag out of a sack, held it up, and asked if she could replace my old bag. She threw my black bag into the trash and strapped the new one to the arm of my wheelchair. "Careful of your grandma's eyes," I heard Cary say. I looked at Harrison. He gripped my hand and giggled. That moment I knew true happiness.

Epilogue

Night sinks down, and I'm transported in the Hoyer lift from my wheelchair to my bed. Deloris says goodnight and turns out the light. I lie thinking about Harrison's hands on my face, hearing the sound of a snowstorm outside my window. His hands become those of my father touching my forehead the last time I saw him. Harrison's eyes have the shape of my mother's eyes, and I think of the misaddressed letter I received from her over a year after she died in October 1994.

"I went to the doctor," it said like a voice from the dead, "and he told me I'll be blind in six months. I can't see so good now. I bump into everything. Sorry I can't come to see you, but Joanie's trying to plan it. Joey never bothers to come see us. Midgie's far away in Texas, and I'm cooped up in Joanie's house. I think of you every day and every night. I wonder if I'll ever see you again."

As had been the case when my father died, I wasn't invited to attend my mother's funeral. Their voices, though, live on in my head. When you reside so completely inside yourself, the prominent voices rise. By turns, I hear the jealous, frightened voice of my mother and the capable, angry voice of my father.

To these voices I add my own. As I hear the labored breathing of the woman in the bed next to mine, I remember one day long ago when I was driving to work, thinking what funny people writers are. Back then, I told myself that I'd never have anything to do with a writer. And poets! They were just too much. It's ironic that now, nearly thirty-two years after the strokes, my primary daily activity is to write poetry.

I think of the misfortunate fact of my brother Joe's own stroke, which he suffered while I was writing this book. Joan told me that he speaks nonsense and tries to walk out of the hospital.

I remember Bill urging me to fight to the end, and all the cards and letters of encouragement he's sent me since he moved to New Jersey.

I remember Arlene's astonishment that first time I raised my eyes. She is now an associate professor at Queens College—City University of New York, where she coordinates the Augmentative and Alternative Communication Program. The work she pioneered at Goldwater has had a lasting effect on the lives of disabled people, not only in the United States but also in other parts of the world.

I recall Joyce's systematic approach to addressing my problems. She is now an associate professor in the Occupational Therapy Department at New York University, where she specializes in clinical research related to stroke rehabilitation. I send both her and Arlene a card at Christmas. Though a small token of thanks for all they did for me, it is my way of telling them that I love them.

I think of George raising Judy alone and never remarrying. Maybe that was his way of telling me that he had once loved me and that no one could take my place. Maybe that was even his way of taking care of me after I'd had the strokes. Nonetheless, I decided this year that it would be good for my self-esteem if I was free of him. I am now in the process of filing for a divorce.

I think with immense gratitude of Minato Asakawa, the vice-president of Kodansha America, who believed in me enough to give me the chance to write my life story. At his direction, Kodansha bought me a computer, which allowed me not only to work on this book but to expand my writing activities. Mr. Asakawa visited me in the hospital and encouraged me to write the truth about my life, no matter how painful that truth is. Recently, he asked me the most difficult question I've had to answer: What would I never have known about myself if I hadn't had the strokes? At first I thought I could not find an answer to such a question. But then I thought of two specific things. First, I don't think I would have realized until it was too late that I was on the road to becoming an alcoholic. Because of the way I was raised and the continual influence of alcohol in my family life, I think I would have followed in my father's footsteps. Even after I learned about the dangers of drinking while pregnant the first time, I continued to drink before and after Judy was born, stopping only during the pregnancy itself. Alcohol consumption was a way for me to dull the pain I'd been feeling all of my life, and if I hadn't had the strokes I think that trend would have continued until the day I died.

My second response to Mr. Asakawa's difficult question has to do with willpower. Before my strokes, I didn't have any clear objective for my life. I could even say that I often took the easy road rather than challenging myself in the face of life's difficulties. I coasted along and thought that one day the right man would appear and make everything all right. Now I know better. Life is only what you make it, as the saying goes. I believe now that to be happy one must have clear goals and objectives and strive no matter what to work toward their successful completion. The strokes gave me a clear choice: work for my happiness or die. For almost thirty years I have struggled on a daily basis. I made the determination to write this book, and despite all the obstacles I faced, it is now finished. Attaining this difficult objective has given me a great deal of pride and hope for my future. I have Kodansha America to thank for that.

I think, too, of Goldwater Hospital. After all, if it hadn't been for the people there who did help me, I might still be thought of as a vegetable. I am thankful for my wheelchair and for the augmentative device the hospital helped me obtain. But I think thirty-two years of hospital life is quite enough. As of this writing, I'm taking the necessary steps toward my next goal—moving into my own apartment. An organization for the disabled called the Queens Independent Living Center is working with my niece, Linda Tropiano, to make this latest goal of mine a reality.

I think of all the wonderful letters I've received from children throughout the United States. One class of fifth-graders in San Antonio, Texas, sent me a binder containing photos of themselves and letters they had written to me. I can't say how deeply their words touched me and how beautiful all their faces looked. I wanted to hug each one of those children and tell them that education is the most important thing in the world. Something I'll always regret is having dropped out of high school. One child named Miguel said that he wished he could write poems like mine. I wanted to tell him that with the proper education he can do anything, including writing poems. I've learned the hard way that you can lose everything else, but no one can take knowledge away from you.

I think of the letter I received in May 1996 from a woman whose mother suffered brain damage in a car accident. The daughter was asking for advice, so I sent her a letter. It reads, in part: "Only we can communicate for ourselves. As long as a person knows the alphabet, let her have a pen and paper! Remember—we will not and cannot be defeated. Don't give in."

As I start to fall asleep, I think of Deloris's wedding in

1996 and how she tried to refuse my gift of a hundred dollars, in celebration of her having found the right man. F-O-R A-L-L T-H-E O-L-I-V-E O-I-L, I spelled out on my alphabet card. F-O-R A-L-L Y-O-U-R L-O-V-E. For it was through Deloris's intervention that the nurses began to treat me like a human being. Though there are still times when I feel belittled by them, the physical abuse I suffered early on has now ceased. They sometimes joke with me and make extra efforts on my behalf. For this I am thankful.

My grandson, Harrison, made me remember how precious life is. Some people live ten years for each year that passes. Others live one year for each of the ten they're given. I hope I live one year for each poem written, for each struggle won, for silence overcome.

Life should never be too easy. If it is, you will be caught unprepared for its awful surprises. At the end of the day, however difficult the place you find yourself in, however terrible your suffering, you must struggle through it with the light of hope in your eyes. That hope may seem unreasonable or mad to others, even those who love you. Ignore them, fight them if you have to, but always *look up for yes*.

Night sinks down, and I close my eyes. Somewhere in the hall, I hear Deloris singing. My poems are my singing. This book is my gift to the world.